Neuroplasticity and
The Default Mind

How to Shape Your Plastic Brain by Forming New Connections to Automatically Get Positive Results, Success and Prosperity

Original Edition

SAGE WILCOX

Neuroplasticity and the Default Mind
How to Shape Your Plastic Brain by Forming New Connections to Automatically Get Positive Results, Success and Prosperity

Copyright © 2018 Sage Wilcox

All rights reserved. **No part of this book may be reproduced, stored in a retrieval system or transmitted in any form or by any means, electronic, mechanical, photocopying, recording, or otherwise, without the written permission of the publisher.**

First Edition, 2018

ISBN-13: 978-1-945290-16-9

ISBN-10: 1-945290-16-1

Library of Congress Control Number: 2018943479

Printed in the United States of America.

Dedication/Acknowledgments

This is dedicated to all the people who are working hard to better their lives and situations, day by day, and in every way. Perseverance and discipline pays off. YOU deserve to make your dreams come true and reach your full potential, and this book is for you. Enjoy!

Deep, humble appreciation to the Divine Source, whom I aspire to grow closer to every day, in faith.

Thanks to all who made this book possible. Also to those who loved and supported me as I worked on getting it published. You know who you are, and I am so appreciative and grateful.

And, most importantly, to the readers. Thank you for taking the time to read this book. I hope you enjoy it and find something inside that resonates and inspires you in some way. If you find any of it beneficial please consider leaving a review. Reviews help more than you know. Thank you! Let's pour our favorite drink, find a comfortable spot, and get started, shall we? Our dreams and goals are waiting to be fulfilled.

Other books by Sage Wilcox:

- *Love Letters from Exes: Proof That Life Goes On After a Break Up and Love Is What You Make It*

- *Get It Up: 101 Ways to Raise Your Vibration, Reduce Stress, Depression, & Anxiety, Increase Joy, Peace, & Happiness and Attract Abundance Automatically!*

- *The 2-Hour Vacation: Let Go and Relax, Reduce Stress & Anxiety, Gain Inner Peace, and Happiness*

- *Until We Fall (A Romance Novel)*

- *The Importance of Doing It: How to Utilize Discipline to Get Out of Bed, and Make Your Dreams Come True! A Guide to Taking Action to Create Successful Habits, Reduce Stress, Anxiety, & Depression & Gain Self-Discipline, Motivation, & Success!*

- *Less Is Best: Declutter, Organize, & Simplify to Reach Minimalism; Get More Time, Money, & Energy*

- *You Had Me at Re: Hello: The Ultimate Guide to Online Dating, Including Tips and Testimonies*

Please visit her website at:
http://sagewilcox.wix.com/books
or
www.findyourwaypublishing.com.

CONTENTS

Preface/Introduction i

Chapters

1. What is Neuroplasticity? 1
2. What Does It Mean? (And Why You Should be Excited About It!) 3
3. Not So Fast 5
   The Science of Neuroplasticity 5
   Fun Facts About Neurons 6
4. How Experiences Change Your Brain 9
   This is Your Brain on Neuroplasticity - Three Analogies 9
   Your Brain is More Plastic During Childhood 11
5. Behind the Curtain – How Neuroplasticity Happens 13
6. The Brain 15
   The Brain's Structure 17
   The Cells of the Brain 19
7. The Mind 21
8. Phases of the Brain 23
   Brain Waves 25
   Infra-Low Waves 26
   Delta Waves 26
   Theta Waves 27
   Alpha Waves 27
   Beta Waves 27
   Gamma Waves 28

9	The Brain and The Body.................................	31
	More Information About Synaptic Pruning..	32
10	Plasticity and Learning – You Can Teach an Old Dog New Tricks...	35
	The Learning Process.................................	36
11	What Can You Do with Neuroplasticity?..............	37
	Recover from Brain Damage........................	37
	Healing the Pain of Depression...................	38
	Addiction...	41
12	Anatomy of Brain Damage	45
13	Genesis, Apoptosis, and Plasticity.....................	49
14	Caveats – A Few Things to Consider..................	55
	How Important is Cell to Cell Cooperation?....	56
	Back to How Your Brain Changes..................	56
	Biofeedback – Also an Important Concept.......	58
	How Biofeedback Works..............................	58
	Heart Rate Variability................................	60
	Do It Yourself Biofeedback..........................	61
15	How to Use Neuroplasticity for Yourself – Putting It All Together......................................	63
16	Eleven Amazing Facts About Neuroplasticity (That Apply to You)..	65
17	The Whole Point of Neuroplasticity.....................	69
18	How to Increase Neuroplasticity in Your Day to Day Life – A Guide for Anyone..........................	73
19	Don't Worry, Be Happy....................................	83
20	The Brains Worst Enemy..................................	87

CONTENTS Continued

21	Steps to New Life..	89
	Reflection...	91
	Asking...	92
	Meditation...	93
22	Simple Practices You Can Do Right Now...............	95
	Conclusion...	99
	About Sage Wilcox.....................................	105

PREFACE

> *"An influx of new research explores how our brains do continue to change and how our very thoughts impact those changes. This natural tendency of our brains to rewire is called neuroplasticity, which can be influenced by both external and internal factors."* ~Tina Hallis

Were you ever told that your brain will decline with age? Or that once your brain cells have died, there's no way of getting them back? As an energy healer and author, I speak with many people from different locations. I found that many of my clients were saying the same thing. They had been prescribed an antidepressant and told that depression and anxiety are just something people have to learn to live with. I decided that I needed to do some intense research on the subject. I studied the subject of Neuroplasticity for over three years and I have **good news for you**: recent research shows that the brain is an amazing organ and it has the ability to compensate for weak links in its makeup. We have known for quite a while that people who suffer from brain damage have the ability to compensate for damaged parts of the brain, but thanks to the (somewhat) recent developments in magnetic resonance imaging (MRIs), scientists, researchers, and doctors can see the brain in action – an extremely exciting development.

In this book, we are going to discuss neuroplasticity, the brain's incredible ability to bounce back from injury (physical and mental), and its ability to improve itself through various activities and lifestyle changes. These improvements can happen quickly – within a few months!

The ramifications of neuroplasticity are far reaching – addiction, anxiety, depression, and some other mental illnesses and diseases can be resolved through these simple changes; changes that will positively affect your physical health as well.

Through our discussion of neuroplasticity, I hope to deliver a message of hope to those who suffer from brain damage or the debilitating symptoms of stress, anxiety, depression, addiction and other misunderstood afflictions. Fear, insecurities, low self-esteem, phobias, etc. You don't have to be a slave to disturbing emotions, or cognitive decline. You don't have to live in default mode any longer. You CAN take back control!

In the last three decades, doctors, scientists, and researchers have made significant advances in the fields of neuroscience and psychology, allowing us better knowledge, understanding, and insight into the brain, the mind, and the psyche of the human species, and living organisms in general. The interesting thing about these advances is that they are not just some esoteric discovery that impacts us from a distance. No. The advances have been significant, immediate and continue to directly impact every facet of our daily lives.

With advances in neuroscience, we have found that isolating disciplines of the brain only gets us so far, then we hit a brick wall. We also instinctively know that there is more to the brain than just being a control center for internal bodily functions. It is also a tool to communicate and connect with the objects that occupy the environment around us.

NEUROPLASTICITY AND THE DEFAULT MIND

Imagine a glass of water. Into this water, we add two color pigments: red and blue. Initially, you see them in three distinct layers, the red, the blue and the clear. In time the molecules of these pigments diffuse through the water and eventually you move from three distinct shades to one homogenous purple suspended in a matrix of water.

What the process of diffusion does to those pigments, our brain does for us by helping us assimilate the essence and information of our surroundings - it helps us to mingle, learn, take on other practices and homogenize our individuality. That is how we grow as individuals, and how we advance as a species.

We can't visually look at it. We can't see it, but what we know to be intangible thoughts and memories are actually physical connections that are made in the brain. The brain, and what goes on within it, is a juxtaposition of what is tangible in nature to what is intangible - look at it this way, holding your pen in your hand is tangible. Thinking and visualizing that same pen is intangible. And there is another twist to it. What we just determined to be an intangible thought, memory, or vision, is actually caused by a physical, hence tangible, mental phenomenon. This phenomenon is the building of neural pathways. When a memory is formed, regardless of its origin, these strands are built. The more we are exposed to this experience, the stronger this fragment becomes, sometimes creating more than one neural pathway to the same outcome. Thus, the next step in true understanding is achieved by combining disciplines and looking at how the mind, brain, consciousness and the universe all work holistically. Neuropsychology is such a combination of disciplines, where we look at the structure of the brain, and the nature of the mind that is built on top of it. But that's theoretical and as important as it is, in the grand scheme of things what flows from it is more important, and that is what lies at the core of our thesis in this book about Neuroplasticity.

The correlation of neuroscience and psychology is of deep interest, as it has the potential to catapult our species forward at rates we can't even imagine and haven't yet seen! This area of neuroplasticity which is not exactly at its nascent or beginning stages is practical, functional and result oriented.

We consider neuroplasticity to be the focus of both the hard science of neuroscience and the soft science of psychology because one influences the other, and vice versa. You can have neurons influence psychology and the way you think and act, and you can have the way you think, and act influence the neural pathways. That is how our species is built - by mimicking. When we mimic a certain act, that builds a neural pathway and slowly, before long, the act we once mimicked becomes our own. It's amazing stuff, and it's about time we learn how to utilize it.

Neuroplasticity comes from the combination of two words, neuro, and plasticity. Neuro is something that we can easily figure out and we know that it has something to do with the brain. But plasticity is not something we come across very often. It means malleability and flexibility - as something made of plastic would feel and look like, but more importantly, behave like. Plastic is flexible and can be molded and shaped.

Essentially, neuroplasticity is the study of how the brain physically changes during one's lifetime to adapt to the circumstances it faces. The change can be structural - the recovery from a stroke, for instance; the change can be environmental - exposure to increased carbon monoxide; or it can be from ideological surroundings and cultural values. The physical brain constantly changes according to the forces it is subjected to, like plastic - thus the reference to plasticity. The brain's ability to respond to injury, stimuli and other parameters are no longer mere theory; there is now verifiable proof.

There have been an increasing number of cases where patients who have suffered from mild to severe stroke were able to rehabilitate their condition and return to full upright biped mobility and ambidexterity because the brain is able to find alternate neural pathways to accomplish the connection between command and execution.

The fact is that the brain is malleable and no longer in contention. Using this fact to rehabilitate injury, improve functionality, advance scope and possibly push the boundaries of what we know, is no longer wishful thinking but rather undeniable reality. That is the direction we will take with this book. We are not focusing on the medical or rehabilitative uses of the knowledge we have gained from neuroplasticity, but rather we are looking at using it to form the basis of creating a life that our conscious mind desires.

This book undertakes to accomplish three tasks in bringing the world of neuroplasticity to the everyday reader and to his or her idea of improving it in a way they see fit. It shows the reader that each person has the ability to alter and adjust the shape and resistance of his or her own mind. This is powerful information because when you alter the shape of the mind, you are essentially changing your destiny.

Each person is born into this world with a certain set of gifts - from the geography of his birth to the geopolitical fortunes of his society. He is even subjected to environmental conditions and ideological pressures. But all those things are mere forces, external to his internal being.

If we can understand that each person is the result of the forces that are acted upon him, on the outside and the forces within him that respond on the inside, then we begin to understand the shape that a man's psyche begins to take. At the center of those forces are the brain and the human mind.

In addition to that, time is the next dimension we need to factor into all of this. Those neural pathways can be determined as a function of time as well. If there are repeated stimuli that cause a memory formation, then those pathways get stronger and last longer. When the stimuli ceases, then the pathways atrophy - over time it becomes inconsequential - something we refer to as 'forgetting'.

Three elements are at play when we think about our existence. Emptiness, substance, and time. All three are represented adequately in the brain and its processes, and these are what mold the brain into what it is at any single point in time. This is essentially the field of neuroplasticity.

A good place to start in the effort to understand the workings of the psyche and the way neuroplasticity works, is by looking at how the brain works and how it is the foundation of the mind, and then how the mind becomes the foundation for the psyche.

The physical melds into the intangible in a way that makes it difficult for us to look at only one thing and not another. The path this book takes is designed to gently hug the contours of the landscape and introduce the facts of the brain, the mind, and the actions that flow from it, and also how it works in reverse. Thus, it is important that we understand how the brain works from a cellular perspective and from a notional one.

INTRODUCTION

> *"Thought changes structure... I saw people rewire their brains with their thoughts, to cure previously incurable obsessions and trauma."* ~Dr. Norman Doidge

Why is brain plasticity so important? Because you have the ability to literally rewire your brain. The brain is designed to adapt. It is designed this way as a survival mechanism. Your brain wants you to be comfortable. It doesn't want you to experience discomfort. This is why phycologists say that approximately 95% of your life is controlled by your subconscious mind. On average, we have about 65,000 thoughts a day. About 75 - 90% of those thoughts are coming to you from your default mind. They are on automatic pilot so to speak. This is great if you've strengthened your neuro pathways and trained your brain to think positively. We need to break away from our preprogrammed way of thinking. Our circumstances, our environment, and the people we spend most of our time with and their beliefs and habits (which they have learned) are shaping and molding our brains. Most of our beliefs are just learned from those we are closest too. You are who you hang out with. You can't fly with the eagles if you are hanging out with the turkeys. You may have heard those sayings before. Even Proverbs 13:20 tells us those who walk with wise men will become wise, yet a companion of fools will suffer. Your life circumstances and what you believe are not your fault because you've been in default mode. You've been going through the motions day in and day out based on all that you have learned, observed, and experienced thus far. But, today is a new day! You no longer have to live in default mode.

What has shaped your beliefs?

This is an important question to ask yourself. Why do you think and believe what you do? Growing up, every time my mother introduced me, to someone new, she would tell them that I am shy and that I never had any self-confidence. I heard that over and over and over. This belief was hardwired into my brain. I am sure that my mother meant no harm. She is an amazing woman. Maybe she thought she was helping me in some way by trying to explain my frightened behavior one time or another, and then it just became the norm. It became a habit. It became hardwired in her brain. My grandmother died when my mother was very young, and her dad was an alcoholic who was abusive to almost everyone in the family. My mother remembers feeling as though she wasn't wanted or loved. My mother said she always promised herself that if she had children she would do her best to make sure they felt wanted and loved. She did the best she could and was deliberate in at least showing us that we were loved. Without knowing it, she had rewired her brain in a good way. She broke the learned behavior of abuse, as well. My mom was very poor growing up, and that poverty mindset was learned and over time was hardwired into her brain, therefore, we repeatedly heard that there wasn't enough money, that money didn't grow on trees, and that "we couldn't afford it". This lackful thinking was hardwired into my brain as a reality and although I worked my tail off, I never had enough money. I always worked two or three jobs at a time, and still couldn't save any money. It was a learned belief that had been hardwired into my brain by repetition.

Do you know someone who is critical a lot of the time? Where criticism seems to be their middle name? Where you can't do anything right? Critical people are difficult to be around. They have a hard time complimenting others. They tend to complain a lot. They like to gossip about others. Well, don't be too hard on them. Their brains have simply been wired this way over time. They were critical one day, and then the following day, and then the next, and without even knowing it, they wired their brain to automatically function, react, and think this way. Their neural pathways are so strong in this area, that it has become a part of who they are. It has become their default mind. It has become automatic. The only way for them to change is to become aware of it and then to work on undoing all that has been done. This takes time and effort, but it can be done. Being critical is not a healthy characteristic to have. If a critical person desires to change their ways, all they have to do is start working on intentionally forming new neural pathways around being positive, optimistic, and supportive. This takes a little bit of effort, but not too much. The minute we start in a new direction is the minute the new neural pathways start to take shape. Use it or lose it. When we stop being critical, by catching ourselves in those moments and immediately replacing the thought, then the neural paths around criticism will start to weaken and disintegrate.

The brain is designed to adapt. You can change your brain for better or worse. If you focus on negatives it will strengthen neural pathways in your brain and make negativity a strong point and a regular part of your everyday life. Negativity will be a default mode for you. If you focus on finding the good in every situation you will be creating, forming, and strengthening neural pathways around being positive and that will become a natural part of your everyday life. The great thing is that we get to choose. We no longer have to just let random thoughts control our everyday lives. We no longer have to have a negative default mode. Worry, doubt, judgments, opinions, lackful thinking, bad habits, etc. can all be replaced and a thing of the past.

However effective you want to be, however, successful you desire to become; or, however large your dreams are, it all boils down to the sequence of actions and reactions which you consciously and subconsciously control. Every action you initiate reverberates into the future to become the history of tomorrow. The actions that dictate your present are the direct result of your mindset. Your mindset is built on the faculties of the mind, which are in turn founded atop the physical brain.

While this book is not to be taken as a course in neuropsychology, its goal is to steer the reader towards familiarity with the nomenclature, terminology, and the workings of the underlying brain, then to familiarize the concept of the mind and how it all ties into beliefs, thoughts, mindsets and actions. What is about to be presented here is highly simplified and designed to take the reader where he stands and does not assume any advanced understanding of neurology or psychology.

The first chapters begin with the physical brain and treat is as an organ - simply that, nothing more. This is a necessary foundation for understanding the mind, which comes on top of the brain. We take stringent care to expound the fact that the mind is not the brain and vice versa. One is tangible and can be physically perceived through sight and touch. On the other hand, the mind has no such tangibility and is entirely notional.

The combination of the different mindsets results in the various characters that individuals can form over the course of their lifetime. There are three elements that go into making and forming a person, which influences and effects the environment around them. The first is the experiences that the person has been subjected to; the second is the beliefs that have been instilled in that person, and finally the effect of compounding.

With an understanding of the brain and all that comes with it, we will then be ready to approach the concept of neuroplasticity. As the name suggests it means that the brain (the neuro part of the word) is malleable like plastic and has a certain degree of flexibility and ability to change and remold itself (the plasticity part of the medical term.)

The brain can be deconstructed into two parts. The ancient brain that is concerned with the basic order of life and the higher brain that gives rise to more sophisticated thoughts and actions. Each has influence over the other, and that influence is manifested in different ways.

Your brain is adaptable, and you can change it yourself! You are literally capable of rewiring your brain and anyone can do it! You can reprogram your brain. Are you excited about this new revelation?! You should be excited!

The brain is designed to adapt. You can and do change and rewire your brain, anyway. Why not be deliberate? When you truly understand what is going on in there, then you can make better choices for yourself. When you notice and focus on negative things, often you strengthen neural pathways in your brain and make negativity a regular part of your everyday life. Negativity will be a default mode for you. If you focus on finding the good in every situation you create, form, and strengthen neural pathways around being positive and that will become a default mode for you. We get to choose. We don't have to let random thoughts, and other people's opinions, that have been lodged subconsciously into our brains, control our way of living.

You may notice that a few points have been repeated throughout this book. Not many, just a few key points. This is deliberate because repetition is one of the most important factors in strengthening your neuropathways. If you find that you get bored with some of the scientific parts of the book, just skim that part and move onto what resonates with you.

I have seen several success stories and many positive transformations take place for my clients once they started practicing and implementing what they had learned. You can rewire your brain to benefit you in the most amazing ways. Let's get started! Your amazing, happy, healthy, fulfilled, successful, and prosperous life awaits you!

1.
What Is Neuroplasticity?

The concept of neuroplasticity has grown in popularity like wildfire. It makes sense that many people are talking about this idea because it is so exciting to think about. However, this makes the phrase neuroplasticity a bit of a "buzz word" so let's nail down exactly what it means.

Neuroplasticity is an umbrella term that speaks about your brain being able to reorganize itself functionally and physically. Neuroplasticity can occur as a result of environment, repetitive thought patterns, habitual behavior, and strong emotions.

The idea that our brains are malleable can be traced way back to the 1800's but this was all theory. The relatively new development of the MRI has confirmed that a malleable, or "plastic" brain is, in fact, a reality. Indeed, science has confirmed that the brain's ability to morph is a reality beyond doubt.

These recent events have changed the traditional belief that the adult brain remains static or was even hard wired after developmental periods that are believed to be important during childhood. Although your brain may be more plastic during your early stages of life, and the capacity for change declines with age, it has been proven that plasticity occurs throughout the course of human life. Anyone can use neuroplasticity to their advantage, even older adults.

Our brains are malleable. According to TheFreeDictionary.com, malleable is defined as:

malleable
1. Capable of being shaped, bent, or drawn out, as by hammering or pressure without breaking.
flexible, moldable, plastic, pliable, pliant, supple, workable.
2. Easily altered or influenced:
ductile, elastic, flexible, impressionable, plastic, pliable, pliant, suggestible, supple.
3. Able to adjust to changing circumstances. Capable of adapting or being adapted. Capable of being changed or adjusted to meet particular or varied needs.
adaptable, adaptive, adjustable, elastic, flexible, pliable, pliant, supple.

We can shape and mold our brains!

2.
What Does Neuroplasticity Mean?
(And Why You Should Be Excited About It!)

You may have suspected that your brain is an incredible organ. Unfortunately, before the advent of MRIs, the only way to study the brain was to extract it – leading to death! So, scientists, researchers, and doctors have only recently been able to trace, study, and research the activity of brains in living humans.

Neuroplasticity means that your brain is incredibly resilient. It is the process that facilitates permanent learning that takes place in the brain – like learning a musical instrument or a second language. That's right, your brain actually changes when you challenge yourself to learn and experience new things repeatedly.

Neuroplasticity means that it is possible to recover from strokes, brain injuries, birth abnormalities, and with more knowledge on the subject people may overcome autism, ADD and ADHD, learning disabilities and have the strength to reverse obsessive compulsive patterns. As we mentioned it can also pull willing participants out of addiction, the terrible feedback loop of depression, and help victims of chronic anxiety and panic attacks find some relief. (We will explore some of these situations in depth later on in this book.)

As you can imagine, what you can do with neuroplasticity can be far reaching. It opens up possibilities for almost every aspect of life, from education, to culture, to medicine. Because the concept is fairly new, we cannot begin to comprehend the limits of this amazing revelation about the brain.

3.
Not So Fast

The same traits of neuroplasticity that make your brain resilient make it vulnerable to negative outside and internal (usually unconscious) negative influences. With a harsh living environment, less than stellar upbringing, or genetic mental illness, neuroplasticity can result in over-reactive, depressive, anxious and obsessive patterns.

The Science of Neuroplasticity

So, what's behind the curtain of this revelation about our brain's resiliency? We intend to deliver an understandable definition of what's going on in your brain when it changes. Being aware of what is happening in your brain is the first step to making positive changes that will result in positive outcomes. You should be excited about this. You can have the future you desire! It's available to you and you have a brain that is designed to take you there.

Your brain is made up of up to *100 billion* or so neurons that make up to 10,000 connections with other neurons. (These connections are also called synapses). Remember this part about connected neurons – this piece of information is very important to get under the hood of neuroplasticity.

We are talking about a process where the brain's neural synapses (connections) and pathways are altered by behavioral, environmental, and finally, neural changes.

Fun Facts About Neurons
- Neurons talk to each other by sending chemical signals across the synapse (the connection between the neurons)
- Neural impulses are an important facet of how the brain works – neural impulses code your actions, thoughts, and experiences.
- These thoughts, actions, and experiences reorganize the structure and function of the pathways that neurons use to talk to each other. This enables the brain to respond to the world around you.
- Neurotransmitter release is also determined by patterns of neural impulses.
- A neurotransmitter is a chemical released from a nerve cell. This chemical then sends a message from a nerve cell to another one, or to a muscle, organ or tissue.
- Basically, a neurotransmitter is a message from one cell to another.

Amazing stuff, right? Here's an example: Neurons send signals across connections. These result in a thought. The thought changes the way that your neurons talk to each other, so you can respond accordingly. If you have a negative thought, a neurotransmitter is released from a nerve cell, sending a message to the muscles in your face, telling them to frown.

Still not clear? Don't worry, by the end of this book, you will be an expert on the inner workings of neuroplasticity.

4.
How Experiences Change Your Brain

This is Your Brain on Neuroplasticity
Three Analogies

Here are three well-known analogies to put the concept of neuroplasticity into perspective.

The film analogy: Think of your brain like blank film. Say you take a picture of a scenic landscape. You are exposing this film to new information. The film reacts to the light it is exposed to, and its makeup changes so that it can record the image of that landscape. Just like film, when your brain is exposed to new information, it changes, so that it can retain the information.

The lump of clay analogy: Say you take a lump of clay and press a coin into it to make an impression. For the impression to be visible, changes must happen in the clay. The shape of the clay morphs as the coin is pressed into it. It reorganizes its makeup as the coin presses down. Just like the clay reorganizes its makeup, neural circuitry in the brain reorganizes, too, in response to new sensory stimulation or new experiences.

The music analogy: Imagine that you just started learning how to play the flute. Learning how to play a musical instrument demands a lot of cognitive, sensory, and motor skills. Think about it – you are reading music and translating what you read into ambidextrous movements that depend on auditory feedback.

With practice, you will develop fine motor skills, nail down time signatures to develop precise timing, and eventually memorize long compositions, among other challenges. This enhances neuroplasticity big time – many levels of the brain are being used at the same time.

When you first picked up the flute, you made mistakes and were very clumsy. Flute players will tell you even eliciting a sound from the instrument can be a challenge for beginners. Yet only within a few days, neural circuits in your brain devoted to fingering your keys will begin to fire repeatedly.

The more your neurons fire, the stronger the synaptic connections become. Think of neurons as friends – the more they communicate, the stronger the friendship and connection is. With practice comes proficiency. Neurons in circuits that are involved with recognizing music tone will connect more distant neurons because different parts of your brain need to speak to each other now. (Including both hemispheres!) The more connections between different areas of your brain, the better.

Your Brain is More Plastic During Childhood

During childhood, your neuroplasticity switch is always on. In adults, it is typically set to off. Don't despair if you are an adult – specific conditions can trigger or enable plasticity, turning the dial back on. You CAN grow your mind as an adult, and the steps you take to tap into plasticity can improve your personal, spiritual, and work life, as well as your health.

Steps like focused attention, hard work, determination and maintaining brain health will kick plasticity into high gear. Lifestyle changes that are good for the body, like exercise and diet also benefit the brain. You will see as you read on that your brain takes cues from your body and your body takes cues from your brain.

The best news? Keeping your brain stimulated might delay the onset of common brain diseases like Alzheimer's and dementia.

5.
Behind the Curtain – How Neuroplasticity Happens

Neuroplasticity involves a lot of processes in the brain. It alters connections between neurons – neural synapses and pathways, and involves changes to neurons, vascular cells, and glial cells.

Neuroplasticity happens thanks to a process called synaptic pruning. This is your brain deleting neural connections that are no longer useful or necessary. The connections that are necessary, in turn, grow stronger.

You may be wondering how your brain decides which connections to prune out. This depends both on your life experiences, and how recently neural connections have been used. When your neurons are underused, they get weak from underutilization and die off through a process called apoptosis. In other words, neuroplasticity and synaptic pruning are your brain's way of fine tuning itself for efficiency.

Neuroplasticity can be brought upon by physical trauma. The body may heal itself from injury, but the brain *adapts*. Many times, physical injury would otherwise result in loss of function in the body. Yet, when someone does lose function after suffering bodily injury, the plasticity of the brain can come to the rescue!

It occurs in two ways:

During normal brain development when the immature brain begins to process sensory information – like when you were a baby and learned to walk. Or through adulthood as an adaptive mechanism to compensate for lost function maxing out remaining functions after brain injury.

6.
The Brain

The brain, the mind, and the psyche are three concepts that confuse most of us into thinking that the terms are interchangeable, and one means the other. I assure you, all are different, all are interdependent to a certain extent, and all behave uniquely over the course of our existence.

The brain is physical. If you were to approach it surgically, you will find that you could pick it up and that it has a physical presence. It has color, texture, and mass. The brain was just the apex of the central nervous system, which spread throughout the body. This system evolved from a very basic and rudimentary purpose over millions of years, to become what it is today.

In essence, the entire mechanism - the brain, the mind, and the psyche are all interconnected in that they are tasked with doing one thing - and that is to fulfill the purpose of our earthly existence.

Most of us, over most of our individual lives, fail to realize that there is a distinct separation between thought, word, and deed. Deeds are the tangible actions that our body performs. The word, on the other hand, is partially tangible and stands at the juxtaposition of being a figment of thought and the reality of action. Finally, there is thought, while being very real to us, it is, in fact, intangible. All three are important and if one is not observant, one could live in a default mode, and not realize or utilize the power available to them.

The brain is part of the central nervous system and sits inside the cranial vault. Every part of the brain is tangible and has physical form. There are four kinds of cells that distinguish the brain, the neurons, and the other essential parts of the central nervous system.

The science behind it may be a bit boring to some, but it's important to get a basic idea of what is going on in order to move onward. Then we can learn how to utilize it and take action in the direction of our dreams. The brain operates by using electrochemical signals and processes to accomplish its tasks of controlling the rest of the body's functions. There are two main functions the central nervous system has to perform. First, it connects sensors to the brain. This connection allows the brain to get information from a host of sensors that the body houses. From temperature sensors, to touch, to taste. Even sight and sound information are part of the information that is sent back to the brain along the nervous system. Once the data is in the brain, the brain decides how to manipulate its surroundings to be able to accomplish what it needs to. Once this decision has been made, the signals are sent back to the peripheral tools in the body to convert thought to action.

For instance, a sensation of hunger sent to the brain could

trigger a thought process that will direct the body to go in search of nourishment. In terms of hunger, there is more than just one trigger. In the case of hunger there is the real call for nutrition which creates a sensation of hunger, and then there is the habit of calling for food at a certain time of the day. Both are the result of neural pathways that have been created over time based on the actions that we subject ourselves to and the external lessons we learn about when it is a good time to eat. The decision process, to get to the point of foraging for food, can be arrived in one of two pathways in this instance. There may be more. The point is that the same outcome can be reached along different paths of the neurons.

The Brain's Structure

The brain is three pounds of gray and white matter with the consistency of blancmange, a french custard. (I'm not trying to gross you out, only trying to get you to have a clear visualization of what it is.) The brain is 75% water by weight and 60% fat by volume. It consumes about the same energy as a 20-watt light bulb and uses 20% of the entire oxygen intake and also 20% of the blood flow. To subtly move that much blood there is approximately 100,000 miles of blood vessels involved in the supply and return to and from the brain. The brain is a resource hog, consuming more resources than any other organ in the body. The gray matter in the brain consists of neurons, and is about 40% of the brain, while the other 60% is white matter, consisting of dendrites and axons, responsible for the transmission of data. There are three functional areas of the brain, the cerebrum, cerebellum, and the brainstem.

The Cerebrum is the largest of the three areas and is divided further into lobes for organizational and observational ease. The four lobes are the frontal lobe, the parietal lobe, the temporal lobe and the occipital lobe.

The frontal lobe is responsible for a vast array of different human thoughts and actions. It is a major part of motor function, memory, judgment, and impulse control. It is also responsible for social and sexual behavior.

The parietal lobe is where the sensory information like touch and pressure is processed. It is also the place where taste is processed.

The temporal lobe holds the areas of hearing, long-term memory, and the ability to recognize faces.

Finally, the occipital lobe is the area for sight.

These are just some of the important areas that have been listed. There are many more that would exceed the purpose of this book if we were to elaborate upon. Needless to say, the lore and belief that we only use ten percent of our brains is patently false.

To be more detailed, there are other areas of the brain that we can separate our study into. There are specific areas of the brain that we know varying degrees of information about but for the most part, science has a long way to go in objectively mapping our brain and understanding how it behaves. But for now, we need to know the following major areas to be conversant in the subject of neuroplasticity. The anatomical location of each function corresponds, correlates, interacts, and of course are associated.

Cerebral Cortex. This part of the brain is instrumental in our ability to remember, pay attention, and remain self-aware. It is located on top of the cerebrum and made up of folded gray matter.

Corpus Callosum. The two hemispheres of the brain are connected by one bridge that allows data to flow between the two. This is the corpus callosum.

Ventricles. In the center of the brain mass is a pocket of cerebrospinal fluid. The fluid is found here, in the brain, and in the spinal column. It is produced by the choroid plexus, also located in the ventricles.

Thalamus. The thalamus is located alongside the ventricles in the center of the brain mass between the two hemispheres. It is responsible for pain management and sensory detection.

Hypothalamus. Regulates the metabolic profile of the person and manages the autonomic functions of the nervous system and controls the activity of the pituitary indirectly controlling body temperature, thirst, and hunger.

The brain's functions that have, thus far, been mapped by western medicine is strictly based on physical representation of cause and effect. This means that when they were mapping the brain they would test one area and see the effect of it and consequently map that function to that area. In each person, the exact location of the control varies, and each person must be mapped to determine where a certain function is located exactly. The approximate area is what is known. The exact area must be individually mapped if surgery is contemplated or by using an MRI conducted with appropriate stimulation.

The Cells of the Brain

There are two broad classifications of cells in the brain and spinal column. The spinal column, although not considered the brain proper, is an extension of the brain in many ways. It is there to help transfer the information to and from the body to the brain. The two types of cells are the glial cells and the neurons.

The neurons in the brain are made up of three distinct sections. The head is the dendrites that connect to other cells. The dendrites are alike tentacles that branch out from one cell body that contains one nucleus. From this same cell body extends an Axon. This Axon can vary in length. Axons carry nerve signals to and from the cell body. At the base of the axon, there are axon terminals.

The glial cells are very different from the nerve cells of the neurons. They have no active part in the formation of cognition. Their only job is to keep everything in place. Glial cells amount to about 90% of the cells in the brain.

7.
The Mind

Everything you just read above describes the physical elements of the brain. The mind, however, is altogether a different business. As much as we use both terms interchangeably, they do not mean the same thing in any way. The brain, as you saw, is a tangible organ that you can touch and feel. The mind, however, is intangible, and is more of a mental construct, than a physical object.

The mind uses memory and extrapolation (which can be referred to as imagination) to develop a kind of pseudo-reality within our head. The mind uses algorithms that are based on occurrences in the real world and then extrapolates them to understand and predict an outcome.

What we retain in our brain and the method in which we retain it is not as simple as we may think it is. For instance, what we see is not what we remember, rather, what we remember is an impression of what we see. That's how it is for most people. For the rare few who remember things as they see it, they are referred to as those who possess a photographic memory.

The same goes for what we smell, and what we hear. It is all subject to interpretation before it is stored. This is true no matter how strongly you believe that you remember things the exact way they occur. Two people can witness the same event but because the brain interprets information before it stores it, they will have different ideas of what happened. Their recollections may be similar, but they will not be the same. Problems can arise when one person thinks what they remember is right, therefore, they think the other person must be wrong. When in actuality, they are both right. They just interpreted and stored the same event differently.

So, we have the photographic memory and the normal processed memory. Photographic memory can be learned, believe it or not, and it can be practiced. The key is that you need not possess a photographic memory, which is on one side of the spectrum, or have a processed memory, which is on the other side of the spectrum. The trick is to have a healthy balance of both. This doesn't mean that you sometimes chose to remember somethings in one way and other things in another way. What it is, in reality, is that you learn to remember all things in raw and processed ways, but you do so, to different degrees, in two different phases of your brain. More on the phases of your brain in the next section.

8.
Phases of the Brain

If you are wondering why we are still talking about the brain when we are supposed to be talking about the mind, well it's because the frequency, or the phases it creates, are very much a part of the mind. It's like radio frequencies. The frequency created by the brain is like that of a radio station creating a frequency so that it can place its programming on top of it. In the brain's case, thoughts and emotions ride on top of the frequency that the brain creates.

In this section, we are not referring to the stages of brain development. The brain is not divided into compartments based on physical separation like the hard drive of a computer. Instead, it is based on different frequencies. The conscious and awakened state, the state that you are in now as you read this, is at a frequency that is relatively lower than your subconscious state. Your subconscious state works at a much faster rate and can hold more.

We are unconsciously operating under the belief that we write our memories and that it no longer matters if we are awake or not. That is untrue. One of the reasons our brains takes up such vast quantities of energy is because our brain is constantly serving it cells with the energy it needs to maintain cognitive functions. If we were to stop the blood flow to the brain for just three minutes or deprive it of oxygen for the same amount of time, what we will find is that the brain is the first to shut down.

The brain is no more static and passive than the heart that beats and has been beating since before the brain formed in the womb, and which will continue beating till the last breath. The brain, on the other hand, will continue to live for approximately three minutes after the heart stops.

In that way, it's like the RAM in your computer. It is volatile memory - keeping what is stored only while power is supplied to it. The moment power is disengaged, everything is lost.

The brain operates on various frequencies that can be observed when it is attached to an electroencephalograph (EEG). The neurons and cells that are in the brain are involved with the passing of electrical energy and with an EEG that is the source of the image that is then produced. If a specific area of the brain is stimulated, then that part has more electrical activity and that is the area that lights up on the EEG.

What we consider as thoughts and what we consider as feelings are both just different wavelengths of electricity that runs through the brain. Your subconscious happens at a much higher frequency, while your conscious occurs between a little over 0 Hz to about 500 Hz. That's about all you can detect. Above that frequency, detection by your consciousness is fairly minimal, but you can feel it. If it goes higher than that, you would not be able to feel it.

For instance, all the things that are going on in your subconscious are happening at a much higher frequency. Different parts of the brain run at differing frequencies. To understand this better we should look at the concept of brain waves. Stay with me. This is amazing stuff, and once you get a better understanding about what is going on in that brain of yours, then you will be able to master it. You will be in the driver's seat, and you'll be able to steer your vehicle in the way you choose.

Brain Waves

Depending on how deep you want to take it, there are numerous wave categories. But for the purpose of this book we will look at just six. These brainwaves are at times referred to as the speed of the brain and it is easy to fall into that trap. What brainwaves are, instead, are the speed at which the electrical impulses pass in repetition through one or through a group of neurons.

Frequencies are measured in hertz. Hertz normally is the representation in seconds. So, for instance, 60 cycles per second, or the repetition of sixty impulses in the span of one second, is said to be 60 Hertz.

The brain technically can't do 0 Hz. And it can't do negative Hertz, either. The slowest that has been recorded is at below 0.5 Hertz and even then, it's a difficult process as detection becomes immensely problematic. The top end hasn't been quite determined yet, although there is a theoretical limit at about 100Hz. All the measurement that happens extracranially is typically detecting the impulses that are happening in the cerebral cortex.

To visualize, imagine this: Take one neuron, from its cell body, across its axon and down to the axon terminals as a wire connected to a switch. Imagine the myelin sheet to be the rubber insulation on that copper wire and imagine the lightbulb at the other end of the wire as the dendrites.

Imagine if you were to turn that switch on and off once every second. An electrical impulse will flow through the wire and reach the bulb, illuminating it. If you increased the amount of times you flipped that switch on and off, the bulb would flash on at a faster rate. The faster rate corresponds to a higher frequency.

In the event, that there is no impulse at all, that is considered death.

Neuroscientists and psychologists have agreed on several bands of frequency. Ranging between just below 0.5Hz and 50Hz with rare but possible frequencies that have been thought to reach 200 Hz for those with intense meditation ability and those experiencing states of enlightenment. We have chosen, as mentioned earlier, six classifications. In some medical circles, there are more, and in some there are less.

Infra Low Waves

Occurs below 0.5 Hz (but greater than zero). This is rarely studied because of the lack of technology in detecting such low frequencies. However, it is theorized to be a state in which the mind is at total rest.

Delta Waves

These are waves that occur between 0.5 and 3Hz. Unlike Infra Low, these are easily visualized in EEG tests and relate to periods of deep meditation. If you invoke these waves prior to learning and study, you will find that memory is easier. But do note, that it does not mean that learning in other frequencies are futile. On the contrary, learning is not just based on the frequency of the mind, it is based on the frequency of the input. If you match input frequency to the frequency of the cerebral cortex, then you have a better absorption rate than you do when they are not in sync.

Theta Waves

These waves are measured between 3 and 8Hz. This is what you get in deep sleep and in some forms of deep meditation. Deeper meditation will put you in the Delta range. Once you are at this level (approaching from a faster cycle down to this), you are leaving the external world of bodily sensations and the environment around you and are able to focus completely internally.

Alpha Waves

Here the waves are measured between 8 and 12Hz. When you practice mindfulness, this is the state you will be in. It is a superior state to be creative and to allow ideas to flow. It is the ultimate definition of the here and now, and the thoughts that come to you in this state are highly imaginative.

Beta Waves

These waves are between 12 and 38Hz. At this frequency, the brain consumes high quantities of energy, requiring constant replenishment of nourishment. But nourishment alone is insufficient as the brain also gets tired when operated at this frequency for too long and requires rest or it is faced with the risk of damage. Any stresses on the brain, including running it at Beta, should be done incrementally and allow the brain to get used to the operating speed before sustaining that speed for too long. This is especially true for Beta and Gamma states.

Gamma Waves

Occurring between 38 and 42 Hz, these waves signify a state of heightened awareness. The brain is able to process input from various channels more efficiently and at a highly accurate state. The thing that conventional researchers find hard to reconcile is that this frequency is above the rate at which the neurons are thought to be able to fire. So, the question that traditional neuroscientists pose concerns the alternate source of wave energy that drives this Gamma state. Some also believe that there is a possibility for spiritual awakening and super consciousness at this frequency.

As a student of neuroplasticity, it is not important that you commit these frequencies to memory. They will come in handy but what you do need to understand is that the underlying functionality of the brain comes from the oscillations of electrical energy that pulses through the neurons.

The Gamma state is really the highest state in which frequencies can go up to levels beyond 200 if practiced meditation is undertaken. Contrary to popular belief, meditation is not the calming of the mind, that is mindfulness. Meditation is about the heightened focus of the mind. At the highest states of meditation, ESP and large quantity data processing can occur.

It is also observed in meditators who achieve these high rates of brainwaves that they can experience time dilation. Time dilation is the mind's ability to interpret time. Without turning this book into a high-level physics text, it is sufficing to say that it has already been proven that time is unique to each of us. There is no such thing as common time. What you see on your watch is not time, it is man's attempt to measure and quantify time, as well as commoditized time for the purpose of scheduling.

When you increase your brain waves out of the gamma range, what you will find is the brain's ability to dilate time, therefore, it will be like fitting an entire hour, day, year, or decade into mere seconds.

All this would not be possible if the neurons, or a bunch of neurons did not exist. Because, as you have already seen, it is the neurons that act as conduits for these electrical impulses.

9.
The Brain and The Body

The brain and the body are more connected than you may realize. Your body tells your brain what to think and your brain tells your body what to do. Consider the brain of a newborn. Right after birth, their brains are flooded with information from sensory organs. (What is this I am seeing? What am I feeling? What is that noise?)

Sensory information travels back to the brain where it is processed. And nerve cells must connect with each other to do this. This newborn's genes tell the pathway to send the sensory information to the correct area of the brain from a particular nerve cell.

Here's another example to clear things up: nerve cells in the retina of your eye send impulses to the occipital lobe of the brain – the primary visual area.

In the first few years of this newborn's life, their brain is growing rapidly. As every neuron in their brain matures, they send out multiple branches. These branches, if you remember from 9th grade biology, are called axons and dendrites. Axons send information out, while dendrites take information in.

To give you an idea of how much more plastic the brain is at a young age, here's a statistic: at birth, each neuron in the cerebral cortex has about 2500 synapses (connections). By the age of two or three, there are 15000 synapses per neuron, twice the amount of the average adult brain. Returning to the concept of synaptic pruning, the reason why adults have less, is because the connections that we don't use become deleted.

More Information About Synaptic Pruning

Synaptic pruning eliminates the weak links – weaker synaptic connections – while stronger connections are kept – and strengthened. What determines which connections get pruned and which become strengthened? One word: experience.

Connections that are activated most frequently or most recently will be preserved. Just like human beings, neurons want a purpose. Unlike human beings, they need to have a purpose to survive. Without a purpose, they die. A neuron's purpose is to receive or transmit information. When they stop doing that synapses become damaged and die.

Plasticity enables the process of both developing and pruning connections – *which means that your brain adapts itself to its environment.*

Think about your neurons as friends. We only really stay connected with close friends we communicate with frequently – the ones we have deep conversations with. We also take time for acquaintances we've just met and might become closer to in the future. But that old friend from high school who occasionally updates her Facebook feed? You have certainly lost touch with her. The connection is gone.

Like your friends, the connections between neurons that stay out of touch will eventually become deleted. Use it or lose it!

10.
Plasticity and Learning
You Can Teach an Old Dog New Tricks

Now that we've covered the logistics of neuroplasticity, here's where things get interesting.

Over the past two decades, we realized that much of what we thought about brain development and cognitive decline is *just not true*. Once upon a time, we believed that the brain's networks were fixed. This is not the case!

Over the past two decades' experts have realized that the brain NEVER stops changing and adjusting. This whole time, we were never giving our amazing, evolving brains the credit they deserved. Here's where neuroplasticity becomes relevant to you. The capacity of the brain to change with learning is also considered plasticity. So, those "brain training" games you can buy for a pretty penny on the app store, or the crossword puzzle, you do every Sunday, could be working out your "brain muscle."
Before we delve more into learning and how it can improve the function of our brain, let's set a definition for the

learning process. Learning is the ability to acquire skills or knowledge through experience or instruction. *Memory* is the process by which this knowledge is retained over time.

The Learning Process

When we first learn something new, the data we discover is stored in short term memory. This affords us the temporary ability to recall a few pieces of information. Short term memory is built upon chemical and electrical events in the brain – instead of structural changes like the formation of new synapses. (Just in case you forgot – synapses are connections between neurons that allow separate neurons to speak to each other). Development of long term memory, as you may have guessed, forms these synapses so crucial for optimal brain health.

You will find out in just a few pages how important learning can be to the health of your brain. But first, let's talk about the different things neuroplasticity can help us with, to illustrate how amazing our evolving brains are.

11.
What Can You Do with Neuroplasticity?

If you've been following along, you're learning about a new concept, strengthening your brain's structure and making it more efficient! Good for you! However, you'd also know that the brain is ever evolving. It cuts off connections that aren't pulling their weight and strengthens connections we have recently used or frequently use. This opens the door for wonderful possibilities for less fortunate people suffering from debilitating physical and mental illnesses.

Recover from Brain Damage

After sustaining a brain injury, your plastic brain focuses on maximizing function, even though the brain is damaged. An interesting study involved researchers observing rats. One area of these creature's brain was damaged. *The brain cells surrounding the damaged area changed in shape AND function which permitted them to take on the functions the damaged cells would have done.*

Imagine recovering from brain damage like re-learning. The brain uses the same neurobiological process it used to acquire the behaviors damaged parts of the brain accomplished in the first place. After brain injury, changes have been seen in the motor cortex as part of the recovery process. These same changes are seen in the motor cortex during its initial learning process.

Heal the Pain of Depression

Neuroplasticity can have a dark and negative side, as well. Our brains are constantly remodeling themselves based on things like behavior, genes, and experiences. We know that behavior, genes, and experiences can also cause different types of depression. So, the link between depression and neuroplasticity is clearer to us now.

Neuroplasticity strengthens neurons sending messages frequently, and synaptic pruning kills neurons that are not sending messages frequently enough. The body feeds off of the brain, and the brain feeds off of the body. For example, say a disturbing thought occurs in your head. As a result, a scowl forms on your face. Your body's sensory organs send a message back to the brain, reinforcing the brain's belief that something is truly wrong. If this happens enough, the connections responsible for these thoughts will grow stronger.

Unfortunately, psychiatrists are only beginning to understand how neuroplasticity plays a part in the development of psychiatric disorders. In the 1980s and 1990s, they didn't put much thought into the ways that the human brain might be affected by depression – or medical treatments for it. It is hard to blame them. If they believed that the brain was a static organ, they couldn't realize that depression, and its negative feedback loop, might be harming the structure of the brain.

Focused on treating symptoms and disorders with medication or therapy, these experts didn't have any sense that what they were doing, and what patients were doing, were affecting their brains. The good news is that the brain DOES keep renovating itself through life. Parts of the brain keep growing new brain cells into adult life.

The choice is yours – you can give in to repetitive, disturbing thoughts that cause neurons sending messages causing healthier emotions to die, or you can employ neuroplasticity in conjunction with therapeutic treatment to help you experience joy in your life again. Whichever choice we choose, will make stronger connections and, thus fire off more often.

Please note that the act of clinical depression is not a choice. It is caused by unfortunate experiences, genetic makeup, or unhealthy thought patterns that somehow formed over the years. But you CAN choose to be more proactive in your treatment with your doctor. (And we don't recommend stopping your appointments with your doctor! This should be used in conjunction with treatment.)

To help you understand how your day to day behaviors have measurable effects on brain function and structure, let us tell you about another study done – this one by the University of London researcher Eleanor Maguire. The study was conducted on British taxi drivers. In England, to get a taxi license, you are required to memorize the map of the convoluted city of London – a massive undertaking that takes many months to accomplish.

Maguire found in this 2000 study that there were physical

changes in the hippocampi of London taxi drivers. Drivers with the greatest enlargement were in those who were driving the longest. Similar studies have found people learning to juggle, or medical students required to memorize huge quantities of facts about biology, chemistry or anatomy have brain changes as well.

What you do can enhance your brain, or it can decrease your brain's functionality – negative neuroplasticity. Currently, forward looking doctors are searching for ways to interrupt negative neuroplasticity, inducing positive neuroplasticity in its place in treatments.

Their goal is to increase brain activity in certain parts of the organ that can foster positive emotions, like the anterior cingulate (the key decision making area), and the prefrontal cortex (the location of planning). If these areas were to strengthen and grow, people suffering from depression might gain a new sense of perspective and be more analytical about their disturbing thoughts.

Say for example, a patient with depression thinks, "My life is hopeless and I'm nothing but a burden." These new strengthened areas can produce counter thoughts like "I have a lot to live for, saying my life is hopeless is catastrophizing thinking, and I can feel like less of a burden by volunteering my time to help those in need."

Meanwhile, while these parts of the brain increase in activity, doctors are working hard to decrease activity in other areas like the amygdala – the brain's fear center responsible for fight or flight reactions.

We've explained how anyone – depressed or not – can incorporate neuroplasticity into their lives to improve them, but physical activity and exercise are great starts if you are depressed and want to have a major impact on neurotrophic factors – chemicals that stimulate the growth and recovery of brain cells.

Yes, when you are depressed, it can take a heck of a lot of motivation to get up three or four times a week and exercise for thirty to forty-five minutes. But focused attention and intense motivation just strengthen the effects of neuroplasticity more!

One doctor, for example, described a patient who had a very difficult early life full of loss and trauma. As a result, she experienced over fifteen years of severe depression and panic disorders in her short, painful life.

The stress was so unbearable it manifested in medical illnesses like severe asthma and colitis. As her depression and anxiety responded just enough to medicine and therapy, she became passionate about yoga.

After practicing yoga two to three hours a day, after just a few months, she reported to this forward-looking doctor that she had achieved a sense of calm she had never experienced in her life before.
The savvy doctor posited that the treatment and the regimen of intense yoga caused changes in the brain, decreasing the activity of the amygdala.

Addiction

Many times, addiction is called a disease. While this helps us to understand the pervasive nature of different treatments, this is a disease that the brain can heal from. Many addicts argue with the twelve-step program epithet "we declare ourselves powerless to our addiction." It is not our intention to discuss twelve step programs, because it does indeed work wonders for many people. But truly understanding the how the wiring of the brain works can help and be of great benefit as well.

When we develop a habit, the brain creates a path in itself (through connections) to support it. As we engage in the habit again and again, the path becomes stronger.

As the brain gets trained to do an addictive behavior, such as substance abuse, alcohol abuse, or gambling, eventually this pathway gets so strong that everything else is excluded. What we mean by this is that when a person becomes addicted to something, the pleasures centers of the brain are hijacked by the addiction.

Eventually, with enough usage, only the addictive behavior can bring the person any sense of happiness, well-being, or sadly sometimes, at least freedom from pain. In that sense, addicts are powerless to their addictions.

The brain can be retrained, and the brain of an addict's biochemistry CAN be rebalanced with practice. So, in another sense we are not powerless. However, the old neuropathways between addiction and pleasure will still remain. This is why twelve step programs strongly advise complete abstinence from drugs and alcohol to addicts.

In a nutshell, we have an opportunity to change our behaviors, but recovery does not remove the addictive thought process. Addicts should hold out hope. Individual neurons might be damaged beyond repair by the substance they have abused, but the brain will heal itself by making new connections to work around the damage. Although there will be an addictive pathway, a pathway that supports recovery can be developed as well. We can create new connections.

The brain can learn to enjoy recovery – it doesn't have to be a painful process that challenges us daily. Addicts can learn to enjoy things that deliver pleasure in sobriety – family, work, and healthy interactions with others, a job well done, a good meal, etc.

12.
Anatomy of Brain Damage

It is estimated that nearly 1.7 million people in the United State are diagnosed with traumatic brain injury (TBI) annually. Another 800,000 people suffer from stroke in the same period. TBIs and strokes are two very different things although it has slowly become acceptable in the general conversation to refer to one and mean the other.

Traumatic Brain Injury is an injury to the head that is so severe that the brain is affected by either penetration of the skull, or by the collision of the internal cranial bone and the brain. In many cases the tissue holding the brain in place is ripped and the brain is bruised and damaged; internal bleeding and swelling may occur, further complicating the matter. In TBI, there is, in many cases, considerable behavior alteration and changes in cognitive ability.

As for strokes, there are three kinds of strokes that we can generally speak of. The ischemic stroke is one where there is a blood clot that blocks the flow of blood to the brain. This causes oxygen and nutrition starvation to that part of the tissue and the neurons in that area eventually die. The second kind of stroke is a hemorrhagic stroke whereas the name suggests, there is a hemorrhage and the area that is affected by the spillover of the blood dies. The third stroke is momentary and is called a Transient Ischemic Attack where a clot temporarily blocks a blood vessel causing some damage before unblocking and returning blood flow to that part of the brain.

As you can see, TBIs and strokes are very different in nature. But nonetheless, they all result in the common outcome where there is damage to the brain, and specifically to the neurons that make up the brain.

We saw in an earlier part of the book that different functions are controlled by neurons located in different parts of the brain. When a bunch of neurons in a particular part of the brain are damaged, then it is reasonable to imagine that the functions that are usually associated to that part of the brain will be impaired. And that is exactly what happens. In some cases, the damage can be worse off than in others and so the levels of motor function deterioration may be more severe.

These two types of damages have something in common. They are both physical in nature. Basically, it's a physical event that affected a physical part of the brain and resulted in impairment that can be detected physically.

Then there is another kind of damage, this time it is not a physical damage to the brain or its components, but rather a non-physical damage. Nonetheless the effects are visible and obvious. This damage is caused by a psychological trauma. It may not cause bleeding and there might not be some form of laceration and swelling, but the damage is, nonetheless, real.

There is one more kind of damage that is similar to physical damage but is more of a toxic damage. This damage is caused by something that you consume. If you were to consume highly toxic opiates, then there could be momentary alteration of the brain. And if you consume chemical toxins the damage could be permanent.

Whether it is physical, psychological or pharmaceutical, the damage is nonetheless real and until now has been considered irreversible. Until now. This possibility of recovery will be discussed and explained in the coming chapters.

Within this ambit there are other forms of damage that you should keep in mind, things like asphyxiation and even hypoxia. Low oxygen levels over long periods of time without the ability to get accustomed to it can also cause permanent brain damage.

Putting aside the specifics, the heart of what we are looking at is the death of a neuron. When the neuron dies, or when it is inefficient, the amount of electricity that it can carry diminishes and so does the brainwaves that we experience.

Until this half of the last century any sort of brain damage, or more specifically neuronal damage was thought to be untreatable and irreversible. Both are wrong, the former more than the latter.

It was recently discovered that brain damage, from stroke, or TBI could have certain success in attempts to stem the effects of the damage.

Scientists first theorize about Neural Adaptation. Neural

Adaptation had been observed for some time before the need to look at remedies for damaged neurons. What was observed in Neural Adaptation is that the brain got used to repeated sensory inputs, and after a short period of time stopped processing them. You've experienced this many times. If you were suddenly exposed to a loud releasing noise, let's say from a jack-hammer at a construction site nearby, you would, at first hear it very loudly. But as the stimuli continued, your brain would slowly shut of its effect. And even though the sound still existed, it would be a lot less for you. I have a relative that lives right next to a railroad track. She said that first week, the sound of the train, and its whistle, woke her up every night and was very annoying. But to her surprise, after a few weeks, she didn't even hear it anymore, and slept right through it.

The same can happen in reverse once this has been established. If while you were 'not hearing' the jack hammer after getting used to it, and if the operator suddenly stopped using it, you could become aware and notice the silence filling the space that was once filled with that annoying noise.

This is the crux of Neural Adaptation and it was the center of keen study. This area has now been supplemented with an even newer area of study which is Neuroplasticity. And it is such an exciting topic!

13.
Genesis, Apoptosis and Plasticity

Neuroplasticity is a fairly new area in the field of neuroscience. It is based on a premise, as the name implies, that there is plasticity in bunches of neurons. This is not to be confused with neurogenesis - which is about the birth of new neurons.

To understand neuroplasticity, it would be a good idea to understand neurogenesis here and then lay the facts and science atop the former. It is also a good idea to understand neuroapoptosis and understand the stages and the lifespan of the neuron.

By understanding the birth to death process of brain cells, we get to appreciate the power and the vulnerabilities of the brain and the mind that relies on it. While neurogenesis is possible, and its existence is now verifiable, it is not without great effort and repetitive process of learning and therapy, that a person who has lost her ability to walk or speak, after an ischemic stroke, must endure.

Neurogenesis

As the name implies, genesis refers to the birth of something new. In this case, it is the birth of new neuron cells. It has been observed, in recent research, that there is a special stem cell that is responsible for the birth of new neurons and that they occur in a special part of the brain. The regeneration of new neuronal cells is a lifelong process and in the event of new learning, new cells are formed on one part of the brain and then are moved to the location where it is needed.

In a way, neurogenesis is a subset of neuroplasticity from the perspective of, and only from the perspective of, adaptation after injury when exercised in a certain way.

In neurogenesis, the brain responds to stimuli, when prompted, by learning a new skill or repeating a new skill and forms a new neuron which it then moves from its place of birth, which is in the frontal cortex, to the place where it is needed. As such, in the event a stroke victim has damage in the area of the brain that is concerned with walking, assuming there is no other damage to the limb concerned, and the ability to balance, then the process of neurogenesis creates new neurons with repeated practice and moves that neuron to the place in the brain that is appropriate for the ability to walk.

The new neurons are born where the neuron stems cells are located. In an adult human being that happens to be in the frontal cortex. Once the cell is born it needs to be installed in the location where it is needed. As such it needs to travel to that location.

There are two methods that the neurogenesis process employs in migrating the newly minted cell to its location.

The first is the use of chemical signals. They are executed with the aid of Adhesion Molecules that are found on the new neuron and old neurons so that when they bind they move along the old neuron until they get to the location that they need to be at. The second method is similar to the first except this time they adhere to the radial glia instead of the neurons themselves and travel to their destination. Unlike previously hypothesized, neurons are not made on location which is one of the reasons it takes time to learn new skills.

Depending on where the neuron was intended to be placed, they will carry different functions. There are more than one kind of neuron. In fact, there are three. There is the motor neuron, the sensory neuron, and an interneuron.

Motor neurons are responsible for carrying impulses from the brain through the spinal column to the muscle group that is in question. The sensory neuron does the exact opposite; it carries sensory information from the extremities and sensors back to the brain for processing. The third kind of neuron is the one that exists to connect the other two. The interneuron is the link between motor and sensory neurons.

Neuroapoptosis

Neuroapoptosis is the death of the neuronal cells in the brain and/or spinal column. Unlike the other cells in the rest of the body, which have comparatively short lifespans - which range from a few days in the stomach lining, to two weeks within skin cells, and 120 days for blood cells; neuronal cells last almost the entire lifetime. The bulk of the cells are produced in the womb before delivery and then a little more are produced after birth. So, cell death is usually at the point when the body dies. This is in normal circumstances.

However, neuroapoptosis can also happen under the influence of alcohol, asphyxia, and brain injuries as we have mentioned. The thing to note at this point is not about how cells die, but how they are replaced. Unlike most other cells, brain cells are not replaced when they die. They are only born when new cells are needed to do new tasks.

As such, premature neuroapoptosis can be a significant problem, especially in the wake of substance abuse, because the cells are not automatically replaced, and it is sometimes not known which function has been lost. Because of the nature of how skills and memories are formed, not all of the same skill keeps the neurons necessary for that skill in the same place. There can be redundancies in other areas as well that the rest of the cells can lean on to get aid, but the difficulty is in knowing which skills need to be polished.

Foundation in Neuroplasticity

Neurogenesis and neuroapoptosis are about the brain cell and its beginning. But neuroplasticity is about how neurons behave in their achievement of their purpose during their lifetime. Each neuron is connected to anywhere from a thousand to ten thousand other neurons, and there are about 100 billion neurons in total. That number stays fairly constant through a person's lifetime - unless certain steps are taken during the fetal developmental stage. It has long been a lore that playing Mozart compositions for a fetus in the womb has a positive effect. For most of the children in a non-scientific study that was conducted where music was played for the full nine months of their pregnancy, it was observed (unscientifically) that the children who were exposed to classical music (not just ones composed by Mozart) had a definite effect. Ten years later the same group of children were observed to have moved further in academics and social engagement than the study subjects who were not exposed to prenatal music and stimulation.

A single neuron is not as useful as when compared to a neuron that is connecting to thousands of other neurons. Their point of contact is called the synapse.

If you think about the brain, it is a physical, albeit a biological object. It is made up of live tissue, which are made up of no less than two different types of brain cells and is fed with oxygen and nutrients. The special thing about brain cells is that they are conductive in nature and they specifically transmit information electrochemically. Dendrites bring information to the cell, which travels down the axon and out via the axon terminals.

A neuron in isolation only has one use - it holds a fragment of information in isolation, and that limited use, without the benefit of the mind placing that information in context or without the imagination to use that information, can be somewhat useless. This is overcome when the neuron connects with another neuron that has other pieces of information. In this same way, each neuron connects to thousands of other neurons, but that connection is not a physical one. There is a gap. This is very ingenious, actually. If the connection was seamless then there would just be information flowing all over the place, and from a practical perspective, that would mean a lot of the information would physically collide with one another and become vastly incoherent and thus useless. Instead there is a gap between the neurons, specifically between the synapsis. This gap acts as a boundary between one neuron and the next, and in that gap neurotransmitters are used to travel from one neuron to the next.

When an electrical impulse moves from the Soma, through the Axon, and down to the terminus, it sparks off the release of vesicles that contain the neurotransmitters. These neurotransmitters then leave the axon terminus and jump the gap into the attached neuron. That neuron could be attached by the dendrite, the axon, or the terminus of another neuron. Depending on where one neuron is attached to another gives rise to a specific term - axodendritic synapse, axoaxonic synapse, and axosomatic synapse. The first term is where the axon terminus is attached to the dendrites, the second is attached to the axon, and the final one is where it is attached to the soma.

With this process in mind we can now begin to explore neuroplasticity and how to go about accelerating it and using it to our benefit.

14.
Caveats – A Few Things to Consider

- The brain has to be in the "mood" for change. If you've gotten this far in the book, you understand the capabilities of a plastic brain and you probably want to explore how they can help you in your day to day life. So how do you get the brain in the mood for change?

- You need to be alert, motivated, engaged and ready for action. When you are ready to give your all into positive change, by maintaining an engaged attitude, then the brain releases neurochemicals that are necessary to enable the change you want – which turns the neuroplastic switch "on" (Don't worry! We give you tips on how to achieve this mindset in just a moment!)

- Being disengaged, distracted, inattentive, or doing things without thinking, will turn your neuroplastic switch off.

- The good news is, the harder your try, the more motivated you are, the more alert your brain is, the better the potential outcome will be, and the bigger the brain change. If you are really trying to master a task, for an important reason, with intense focus, the change you experience will be greater.

What is changing in your brain, during your periods of intense focus, when you master a new task? You may know by now that what changes are the strengths of connections of neurons, engaging together, moment by moment, in time. The connections being made get stronger and stronger.

- The more something is practiced, the more connections are changed and are made to include ALL elements of an experience – sensory information, cognitive patterns and movement.

- Changes driven by learning increase connections – cell to cell cooperation that are crucial for increasing reliability.

How Important is Cell to Cell Cooperation?

Imagine a football stadium chock full of fans clapping at random. Now imagine all of these fans clapping together, in unison. The clapping is louder, more cohesive, and conveys a stronger message. Just like these football fans, the more coordinated your nerve cell teams are, the more powerful and reliable their behavioral productions will be.

Back to How Your Brain Changes....

- Initial changes are temporary. The brain records the initial change, then figures out whether it should make the change permanent or not. If the experience changing your brain is novel enough, or if the behavioral outcome is important (like a first experience doing drugs sends levels of dopamine spiking) the change will be permanent, whether it's good or bad.

- Memory controls most learning (we talked about the definition of learning and memory before, remember?) When you a learn a new skill, the brain takes note of the novelty. It remembers the great attempts you had at learning and tosses out the not so good ones from memory. Most importantly, the brain remembers your last good attempt at learning, makes adjustments to itself, and improves progressively.

- Learning is imperative to improving your life with neuroplasticity. Every moment of learning gives your brain an opportunity for it to stabilize. This reduces the disruptiveness of background "noise" interfering. Every time your brain makes a connection stronger, to advance your skill, it weakens connections of neurons not used at that specific moment.

- So, if you want to reduce communication between neurons that cause anxiety, you can focus on learning piano, for example. As you learn piano your mind quiets. As your mind quiets the connections between the neurons causing your anxiety aren't being used, and will eventually die, because the connections for the neurons powering your new skill are so much stronger.

Biofeedback – Also an Important Concept

As you've read, your brain controls your body, but your body controls your brain as well. It's an endless loop that works both ways. Biofeedback is the activity in your brain that changes every second depending on your body and what it is doing.

You can also alter the way your brain functions with conscious biofeedback. Although machines like a finger monitor can give you a precise measurement of your biofeedback, they aren't necessary. You can change the way your brain functions by simply paying attention. Your thoughts don't have to rule your life. Paying attention to your body and your mind's relationship can have tremendous benefits for your thoughts, emotions, feelings and stress levels.

Your brain notes what is going on with your body and how you feel – your heart rate, your muscle tension, the amount of sweat you are producing and the shallowness of your breathing. Once you become aware of these factors you are ready to do conscious biofeedback. (Meditation is an amazingly efficient way to be able to achieve this type of awareness.)

How Biofeedback Works

Your brain is constantly receiving signals from your body. Your brain depends on your body to tell it about the environment and it also tells your brain how to feel and think. The body does this by sending sensory information to your brain. Your brain interprets the information from your senses as feelings, adding its "special sauce" to produce emotions.

A really empowering fact, you should know, is that there is a difference between feelings and emotions.

A feeling in the pit of your stomach, for example, could mean you are hungry (feeling) or anxious (emotion). All your brain knows is that your body is telling it about a feeling – it is sending it a sensory signal. Think of this signal like your vehicle's check engine light. This light isn't extremely useful to you in your car. You're alerted that something is happening to your car, but the "check engine" light doesn't help you by telling you what it is.

Conscious biofeedback entails doing a self-assessment of your feelings to help your brain distinguish these vague signals. Physical sensations, like aches and pains, tight muscles, or a queasy stomach, may be triggering an emotion from your brain which could be appropriate or not. That's why you need to interpret and influence the physical sensations that get sent to your brain.

Take our depression example from before. When you are depressed, you tend to frown, scowl, or exhibit withdrawn postures. These increase feelings of tension. The physical symptoms of depression, like muscle tension, increases anxiety and lowers heart rate variability which reinforces the depression. A vicious cycle.

People generate negative types of biofeedback unknowingly, like with depression. Frowning or scowling expressions, or timid, withdrawn postures, unfortunately, increase feelings of tension. The key is being aware of it and knowing that your brain is plastic, therefore, you can slowly trick it into creating other expressions. For example, smiling sends good feelings to the brain. How amazing is that? The simple act of smiling sends feel-good messages to the brain.

Heart Rate Variability

Low heart rate variability is a bad thing. Here's a quick and dirty explanation so you can get started on making positive changes, instead. Heart rate variability, HRV, is the change in time between heartbeats. It's regulated by the parasympathetic nervous system – the calming breaks of your body, and the sympathetic nervous system – the gas pedal that revs things up.

When you inhale and exhale deeply, information travels along something called a vagus nerve, causing your heart rate to slow down, increasing HRV. Sympathetic (excitatory) nervous system activity increases your heart rate, decreasing HRV. When you feel depressed, the vagus nerve shows less activity, meaning your heart does not change speeds as much.

To raise HRV, try exercise – the change in time between heart beat increases while heart rate increases.

We mention HRV because it has strong ties to emotional and mental states, as well as bodily functions.
HRV patterns are significant. Emotions like stress, anger, sadness, and anxiety cause the time in between heartbeats to be disordered and chaotic.

Emotions like gratitude, or love, cause your HRV to be ordered and rhythmic. Good to know, right?

You can learn to regulate HRV with biofeedback, reaping emotional benefits like improved cognitive function and memory, reduced anxiety, blood pressure and cortisol levels, and improve your mood and physical stability.

Do-It-Yourself Biofeedback

You can take back control of your emotions and influence your own body through your own actions. Here are some tips to stimulate the vagus nerve.

- Next time you feel anxious, overwhelmed, or stressed, fill a sink with cold water and splash your face, stimulating the vagus nerve and increasing HRV. Increased HRV means negative emotions will subside, bringing on a calmer, more relaxed mood.

- Use music to increase HRV – while listening to music works, producing music has an even more powerful effect on your HRV. That's because playing and listening to music engages most of the limbic system – the center that governs emotions.

- Trick your brain with a fake smile. Your brain is smart, but when it comes down to it, it can't tell if your smile is provoked, or genuine. Keep a gallery of funny memes on your cellphone, take down a list of jokes that make you crack up, or remember silly situations you were in. When someone or something makes you laugh, make a note of it and read this list often. It will do wonders.

- Send a powerful message to your brain with posture – Standing up straight, in a confident posture will elicit feelings of decisiveness and confidence in your own thoughts and beliefs. But there's more to the story. Posture is a source of feedback, not only to others around you, but to your brain. For example, standing up straighter increases energy, while slouching decreases energy. If your posture is withdrawn, your brain may start to believe that

- your body is sending it a message that you should be feeling a negative emotion.

- Calm your face – Just like you can trick your brain into thinking you are happy when you smile, when you furrow your brow and tense the muscle in the middle of your forehead, your brain thinks you are worried and upset. Take a minute, every now and then, to tell the muscles in your face and forehead to calm down and relax.

- Relax your jaw and tongue – when we are stressed we clench our teeth and tense our tongue. Unfortunately, after enough stress, this can become a habit. Whenever you are aware that your jaw and tongue are clenched, consciously loosen your jaw, open your mouth and wiggle it around. Yes, relaxing your tongue will actually calm your mind.

- Change your breathing – taking long deep breaths into your stomach slows your heart rate and activates the calming parasympathetic nervous system. To do this effectively, put your hand on your diaphragm while taking slow, full breaths. Fill your belly up, count to six, moving your hand in and out with each deep inhale and exhale.

Try clenching and relaxing your muscles – When you clench your muscles then relax them, you can realize the difference and enjoy it. To do this take a deep breath, then flex a tense muscle for a few seconds. Hold it for a moment, flexing it, exhale, then relax the muscle. Important muscles to try this with include the face, hands, neck, back, stomach and glutes. An example would be to lift your shoulders up to your ears, hold the tension, and release.

15.
How to Use Neuroplasticity for Yourself – Putting Everything Together

At this point you might be saying to yourself, "Well that's great, but I don't have brain damage, I don't have clinical depression and I'm not an addict or a substance dependent individual." You don't have to have major problems or issues to inspire you to move towards a better and happier life. Have you ever tried to change something about yourself but doubted your ability to do so? Do you ever feel stuck in your old ways, sitting down in front of the television every night instead of stimulating your mind and improving your emotional health? Do you have any long-term goals you'd like to acquire? Do you wish for some better habits? Do you wish you had the discipline required to make a big change? Does life just seem too hard sometimes? Maybe you're worried that it is too late to change. Or that it's too hard.

Well I'm here to tell you it's not! It's not too late to change! And it's not too hard. What if I told you, that it's actually very simple.
Our bodies are in a constant state of flux. It doesn't take years of studying to come to the realization that your habits

and lifestyle have an impact on how your body turns out. If you are a workout enthusiast, and run miles a day, in between long gym sessions, your body will grow muscles, stability and overall strength.

It's not farfetched to come to the realization, after reading this far, that the brain can also improve itself and rejuvenate itself – at any age. Just a reminder, the brain is capable of forming new neurons and connections and then functions in the brain change too. And what we do from day to day influences the functioning of our brain.

Just like improving your body takes hard work and dedication, rewiring your brain takes active participation and conscious effort. Again, the more you repeat a certain behavior, the stronger the corresponding pathway in the brain will grow. The more you pay attention, the more you practice, the easier taming your brain becomes!

The following chapters will give you even more information and show you simple steps you can take to put this all together and make it work for you. Everyone can do it!

16.
Eleven Amazing Facts About Neuroplasticity (That Apply to You)

1. Education increases the number of branches among the 100 billion neurons in the human brain, and the amount of connections your brain can make. Taking time to learn new things, therefore, actually increases the volume and thickness of your brain. Just like muscle, your brain needs mental workouts. And just like exercising can prolong your life, brain exercises like logic puzzles or even a trip to a museum can slow mental decline. Learn new things.

2. Physical exercise is good for your brain, too! It promotes new neuron creation in the brain – a process called neurogenesis. Neurogenesis helps the brain's balance system, allowing it to function as a whole.

3. Using both sides of your brain is good for you. When we get old, we tend to shift cognitive activities from one lobe to another. And as we age, we use both hemispheres for tasks that used to take place in only one. Our plastic brains

might be compensating for weaknesses from cognitive decline.

4. Before you go to type out that email, know that handwriting strengthens your motor capacities and even adds fluency and speed to reading. Hand write a letter to someone you love.

5. As we think, the *brain physically changes*. We know this because it is possible to measure these changes electronically. Because we can measure these changes, paralyzed people can move objects *with their thoughts and interact with computers*.

6. Your little league softball coach was right when he told you to visualize a home run. You can improve performance through visualizations. Imagination and action activate the same parts of the brain!

7. Being left in the dark can be good for you. If for some reason you were to wear a blindfold for two days, your visual cortex would reorganize itself to process sound and touch. Take the blindfold off, and your visual cortex will stop responding to sound and touch within twelve to twenty-four hours.

8. Meditation does more than relax you. During a study with Buddhist monks and volunteer students, the Buddhists, who had trained in meditation, had their brains studied along with the regular volunteers. The clinical equipment used to examine the brain activity determined that in the monks, powerful gamma waves were activated much more than the students who did not meditate regularly.

Even when both groups weren't meditating, the monks

still showed a large increase in their gamma signal. These intense gamma waves signal higher mental activity and heightened awareness. Focus, memory, learning, and consciousness are enhanced in the neural coordination of practicing meditators.

9. Playing music does more than just make you look cool. Gray matter volume is the highest in volume in professional musicians, as compared to medium level and amateur musicians, and lowest in non-musicians in brain areas such as anterior superior parietal areas, motor regions, and inferior temporal areas.

10. Learning to juggle isn't just for clowns. Getting juggling training can increase the amount of gray matter in the occipitotemporal cortex within just seven days of training.

11. Abstract art isn't just for snobs. Learning abstract information triggers changes in the brain. Medical students who have to consume a large amount of abstract ideas showed changes in the posterior hippocampus and the parietal cortex induced by learning. These are the regions involved in memory retrieval and learning.

17.
The Whole Point of Neuroplasticity

The whole point of neuroplasticity is that your brain is adaptable, flexible, and plastic. The phrase "use it or lose it" is right on. When you learn something new, new connections are made in your brain, and the more you do this new activity, the stronger the connection gets. New neurons are made with each new activity and experience that you discover and pursue.

It is possible to have thousands of neurons in the space of a red bean since each neuron can measure between 4 and 100 microns in diameter. Neurons come in different sizes and can range from a fraction of an inch to several feet long. Again, neurons are nerve cells that carry nerve signals to and from your brain at up to 200 mph. These neurons are supplied with a rich supply of oxygen and nutrients because the activities of the neurons take up a tremendous amount of energy. If, in the event, there is an injury and the affected area consists of parts of hundreds of neurons, the body would have to find a way of repairing it.

There are two ways of repairing it - one direct and the other indirect. The indirect method first. In the indirect method, whatever skill or memory that has been lost - with the death of that group of neurons - can be re-learned. And in that event, it is possible that, with significant effort expended, the brain will create new neurons and send them to the needed area. But this is not a direct replacement. The new neuron would go to the area of the old neuron, but it would not have the same connections that the old neuron had. The new neuron would have to make up the connections that the old neuron had, and that would take a lot of effort and time. But the important thing is that it can be done.

The second method utilizes neuroplasticity. In the event of minor damage, or in the event of minor degradation, the brain, instead of creating new neurons, makes use of the old one just by forming new connections in different locations. If there were four neurons, for instance, A, B, C, and D, and in this example, A connects to B, which connects to C. D, however, is not connected to anything here except to other neurons and is a replica of B. In the event B were to become defective or die, then the crux of neuroplasticity would be that A and C would now form new synaptic connections to D.

It is also possible that entire neurons cannot get damaged. The only part that does get damaged is maybe a dendrite or two and possibly one of the axon terminals. In this case, it is possible to lose a connection with another neuron and so the dendrites grow to make a new connection. This also a form of neuroplasticity.

The whole point of neuroplasticity is to be able to keep thoughts and functions in the brain intact in the event of two things. One, if there is damage to the neuron. And two, if you want to change an ingrained habit and override something that you have already learned. A good way to do this is to erase past connections and create new ones. This is the whole point of neuroplasticity.

I know the science behind neuroplasticity can be somewhat overwhelming, but the very important point I'm trying to make with this book, is that you can change your brain to become a new person, better than the one you were yesterday and significantly better than the one you were a year, or even a decade ago. This was a crazy and exciting revelation for me. No longer did I have to feel that I wasn't smart enough, or that I'd have to settle with things as they were. There is proven science behind this, now. We can train our brains in so many positive ways.

When you understand neuroplasticity, and you understand the underlying neuroscience behind it, what should become apparent is that you can be whomever you want to be because everything you are boils down to connections of synapses and the chain linking of neurons. And because of the new science of neuroplasticity we are now able to conclusively determine that it is entirely possible to change who we are from thoughts, to mindsets, to actions, and to behaviors. All of which are literally anchored in the chains of neurons and synaptic connections.

We as conscious beings want a say in who we become and how we want to be. It turns out we can control this with neuroplasticity. All we need is the knowledge of how to do it and the will to repeat the steps needed to get it done. In the next chapters, we will lay out the steps you need to take in order to get your brain in the mode that promotes neuroplasticity. This is exciting stuff! Be prepared to see positive results in your life and fast. Your brain wants to give you what you want.

18.
How to Increase Neuroplasticity in Your Day to Day Life
A Guide for Anyone

These tips and tricks will not only increase your positive brain power, it will make you a more interested, well rounded, happier person. Participating and engaging in new activities, learning new skills, and interacting with other people will have beneficial effects across the structure of your brain.

As you challenge yourself to think about new things and to think in new ways, your life will be enhanced, and your brain will be more proficient. Juggling, tango dancing, and three-dimensional puzzles for example, are easy ways to turbo charge your brain's plasticity due to the simultaneous demands on both hemispheres of the brain.

If you can learn one new thing every day, your brain structure will change. Your thought speed will improve, as well as your decision-making abilities, and you will have an enhanced capacity to comprehend events as they happen around you. The implications are far reaching – this has obvious benefits to your work life, your spiritual life, romantic and social lives as well.

With the advent of the internet, chock full of free courses and certifications, meetup groups you can join online and the massive number of free books and music you can consume online, pushing yourself to try something new has never been easier.

Here are some activities you can incorporate into your daily routine that will enhance positive neuroplasticity.

1. *Faced with something unfamiliar or difficult? Go for it!*

Who doesn't want to speak multiple languages or master a new technique they have been admiring? Whether it's learning a new computer program, engaging in a new hobby, or even incorporating a new physical activity into your life, you will find that once you put the effort into learning one thing, a snowball effect will occur. Picking up on new exciting challenges will become easier and easier.

Bonus tip: Try to find activities that use both hemispheres of the brain

The right hemisphere of your brain is the center of holistic reasoning. It recognizes patterns, interprets emotions and nonverbal expressions.

The left hemisphere of your brain is the center of logical thought processing. It sequences analytical thought and is responsible for detailed object perception.

Here are some examples of the left hemisphere and right

hemisphere at work.

Reading: The left hemisphere reads words sequentially from left to right. As the left side decodes each word, the right hemisphere interprets the contextual meaning of words at the same time.

The right hemisphere allows us to see many things at once, painting a whole picture of the details gathered by the left side of the brain.

Interestingly, the left hemisphere controls the right side of the body, while the right hemisphere controls the left side of the body.

With Our Powers Combined...

You might see why doing ambidextrous activities, like juggling or playing music, strengthens your brain's abilities. When your whole brain is thinking, the size of engaged areas of the brain increases. Whole brain thinking improves physical coordination, enhances creativity, and improves your instincts and intuition.

2. Focus Focus Focus!

When you *fully* focus your attention on objects, new information, or events, your neuroplasticity is heightened. When you place all of your attention into a conversation, not only are you more pleasant to speak with, your capacity for empathy increases, and the information you take in, when you mindfully focus, gets absorbed into the brain, causing new and stronger connections.

You may have heard the term mindfulness, and blew it off

as a buzzword, but paying attention to the details of your environment, or say, the nuances in the conversation with a friend, your brain gets a supercharge.

When you see new information, reflect on what you are learning and taking in. So, when you follow tip one, (which, of course, you will!) and learn something new, try explaining what you have learned to someone else, or imagine you are explaining this information to someone. This will make the new information "stick," and every new bit of information creates new neural pathways in the brain. When you reflect and recall this information, those new neural pathways are strengthened.

3. Live Like a Local

Ever noticed when you travel, even if you haven't done much physical activity, you feel more exhausted than you normally would at the end of the day? That's because you are taking in a substantial amount of detail exploring a new environment.

When you do have the opportunity to travel, live like the locals. Rather than going to touristy places, try to adopt the practices and customs of people you encounter during your trip. Go to historical sites, explore different religious centers, visit museums, take guided tours, and focus your attention fully while exploring.

Of course, we can't always be traveling, but you can change your attitude towards your daily environment as well. Instead of just walking from point A to point B, utilize mindfulness. Investigate your surroundings and look for novelties you otherwise would have missed. Feel the weight of your feet as they take each step. Think about where you are esoterically.

If you are an avid biker or walker, you might have a favorite trail or neighborhood you enjoy traveling through. Challenge yourself to choose a new location. If you're feeling brave, put your phone down, for a while, and navigate on your own.

When you encounter new people on the street, in your daily life, engage with them by smiling or nodding. Or, if you have time, stop and introduce yourself. Engagement and novelty are great for the brain.

4. Build Your Body to Boost Your Brain

Exercise improves your circulation and reduces stress, improving the blood flow and oxygen sent to the brain. For a proportionally small organ, it is amazing to note that the brain uses 20% of the oxygen we take in.

If hitting the gym seems intimidating, take a walk for thirty to forty-five minutes, doing what we suggested in tip two. Exercising three to four times a week for thirty to forty-five minutes is optimal exercise for your brain. For a bonus one-two punch, watch an informational program on television while you work out to encourage whole brain thinking, or listen to a Rosetta stone CD, and learn a new language, while you walk.

5. Meditation Makes Everything Easier

We have already mentioned that meditation holds many interesting beneficial effects on the structure of the brain, increasing the thickness and strength of the frontal cortex of the brain – something that decreases in size as we age. Meditation reduces stress and cortisol, boosts immune system, and makes all of the other tips we have mentioned easier.

6. Cultivate Stimulating Friendships

As we get older, we tend to seek out things we are familiar with, namely friends. Although we may share common interests, these friendships are still stimulating. If you are looking for a new friend group, start with a common interest – like a book club. Exchange new ideas while you share the appreciation of the activity you all love.

Sharing, teaching, and engaging with others all boost new neural development. Empathizing is important as well. The act of mirroring the emotions of another encourages our brains to explore new perspectives and emotions – enhancing neuroplasticity.

7. Laugh at Life and Celebrate

Staying in a positive mindset is essential for brain training to really be effective. You need to feel positive for the motivation to challenge yourself, and you should put yourself into a positive frame of mind, so your brain is in the right "mood" before any brain training exercises.

Laughter is naturally healing, it reduces stress and produces an overall sense of well-being and will boost your positive neuroplasticity as well.

Ever notice while watching a football game, that after scoring a touchdown, a player often does a victory dance? Come up with your own victory dance, to do, to generate a positive feeling of excitement after every healthy habit you do, whether it's small or large. Just like a provoked smile can trick your brain into believing you are happy, generating a feeling of excitement is a provoked reward that will eventually become natural.

Jump up and down, think of something that made you laugh (keep an ongoing list), watch funny videos, look at pictures from parties and celebrations, remember accomplishments that you are proud of, throw your hands in the air, anything to encourage those butterflies in your stomach that you feel when you are truly celebrating something great. Praise life and all that is good about it! Every step you take towards enhancing your life is great too – so celebrate! After enough celebration, your brain will eventually make the connection that you should feel excitement after you complete a new, positive habit – even one you might have once felt would be too difficult to complete every day.

8. Feed Your Brain

The brain sure takes a lot of oxygen and it eats a lot too. For a small organ (weighing in at only 2% of your body weight) it consumes up to 20% of the nutrients we take into our bodies. Here are some delicious choices that are great for brain growth and slow the rate of cognitive decline.

-Walnuts and raw almonds – these irresistible nuts are great for the brain. Kick the day off right by substituting almond milk in your breakfast cereal.

-Dark Chocolate – You may have heard that dark chocolate can actually be good for you. Well, it's good for your brain too. The flavonoids found in dark chocolate improve your circulation, putting oxygen on the fast track to your brain. We recommend dipping frozen bananas into melted dark chocolate morsels for a low calorie, delicious healthy snack.

-Leafy, dark green vegetables – You don't have to be a "juicer" to slow the rate of cognitive decline. Just incorporate veggies like kale, spinach, romaine lettuce or collards into your diet. One suggestion we have is "kale chips" – try tossing some fresh kale on a baking pan and sprinkling some sea salt on it if you can't stand the idea of eating raw leafy vegetables.

-Cruciferous vegetables – While we are on the subject of veggies; broccoli, cauliflower, brussel sprouts and cabbage also slow the rate of cognitive decline. You can steam these and sprinkle on some low-fat Parmesan cheese for a delicious snack.

-Omega 3's – Don't forget the amazing capabilities of Omega 3's. These have various health benefits and are great food to feed your brain. Studies have shown, for example, that Omega 3's can help manage manic and depressed episodes associated with Bipolar Disorder, and not only that, they are great for anyone looking to improve their brain. Try salmon, sardines, lentils and flax seeds if you want to get Omega 3's straight from the source. If you can't do fish a couple of nights a week, you can opt for supplements.

-Monosaturated fats – Doctors have been telling us for ages that monosaturated fats such as olive oil and avocados are good for us. But they can also slow down the aging of the brain, improving vascular health and circulation. A hard-boiled egg white (yolk removed), with some mashed avocado inside, is a low-cal treat you can try if you get hungry before dinner.

-Berries – Often referred to as "superfoods" (although the jury is still out on exactly what a superfood is, and if we should consume too much of one food item), berries are undoubtedly good for the body and good for the brain. The more colorful your selection of berries, the better. Try mixing berries into half a cup of plain Greek yogurt for breakfast.

-Water – Dehydration leads to impaired cognitive function, and water is just plain good for you. Buy an inexpensive reusable water bottle, fill it at night and keep it next to your bed so taking a sip can be the first thing you do in the morning. Now *that's* a brain hack! Water is the best beverage you can have in the morning, before your coffee or hot chocolate. When I think of the importance of water, I like to think of house plants. Have you ever been behind on watering one of your house plants? We are like plants. When we get low on water, we tend to get droopy and tired. The good thing is, once you finally water your thirsty plants, within a few hours they perk up, straighten out, and look as good as new.

Dietitians and doctors have been advising us to eat more fruits and vegetables and less meat for a while. Nevertheless, this can be a difficult endeavor for many. The idea of learning a musical instrument, going to a museum, or meditating might seem appealing to you, while incorporating a healthy diet and exercising might seem a bit more challenging. But it's important to set the stage for your brain to be able to flourish. The right diet and exercise will put you on the fast track to positive neuroplasticity, so your brain can improve even faster and more efficiently. If you can't stomach the idea of changing your diet (no pun intended) try exercising first. You may find that exercising, after a while, will put you in a better state of mind where you want to care for your body. At this point, making healthier diet choices will come a lot more naturally. Note: People who have rewired their brains to eat healthier, often cannot go back to processed, unhealthy foods.

19.
Don't Worry, Be Happy

Would you like to increase the areas of your brain structure that generate positive thoughts and emotions? Well, you can. Frame your thoughts positively enough, when it occurs to you, and before you know it these areas of your brain will reward you by generating positive feelings.

Warning: Engaging regularly in negative thinking increases the areas of your brain that produce more negative thoughts. Negative thinking can become a bad habit, but once you become aware of it, then your thinking can become deliberate. Being deliberate with what you think, is extremely freeing.

Easier said than done, you may be thinking – especially if you are in that negative mindset already. But if you follow these simple tips, you will notice a snowball effect, in a positive direction. Meditating can help make you more aware of your thoughts. Being mindful of your surroundings will make you more thoughtful. Keeping your mind occupied with puzzles, learning, and new activities will take your mind off negative thoughts and feelings, as well.

Since this may be the most difficult task on the tip list, here are some ideas for you to start feeling good, which will raise your vibration, and cause more good feeling thoughts to automatically come into your experience.

Keep a gratitude journal. Do this religiously. Every day, write down five things you are grateful for in a private notebook. At first this might be a challenge to do. Do it enough, though, and being grateful will come naturally. Eventually, you will find it hard to limit yourself to just five things to be thankful for.

Stressed out about your heavy workload? Try "I am thankful for the abundance of work today."

What you are doing, is deliberately giving your brain another way to look at things. Some call it tricking your brain, because your brain literally can't tell the difference between reality and what you tell it. It's such an amazing thing! And once you figure out how to master your brain, your life can be amazing in every way.

Depressed about the rainy weather? How about "I am grateful that the rain is cleaning the ground and watering our earth?"

Really, anything you are feeling down about can be flipped around into something to be grateful for.

Suffer from negativity? This one might be tough, but how about "I am grateful that some days I feel down, because those moments help me appreciate good days, or just normal days, more than those without."

Are you haunted by memories of abuse, trauma, or sometimes feel like you haven't been dealt a fair hand in life? Take positive actions. Give to others what you wish you had been given and you will start to heal. For example, a victim of sexual assault might have been failed by the system. This survivor can start healing by volunteering for a domestic violence and/or sexual assault shelter.

Remember that we are not disturbed by the things around us, but by the thoughts we have about them. Your significant other might come home two hours late for dinner. You can launch into an argument with her before letting her explain, or you can express your concern and ask what happened, reacting after some time has passed by. The choice is yours. You can think in ways that will make your life and relationships more productive.

Be patient with yourself. Learning new things and challenging yourself to enhance positive neuroplasticity may result in some failures. It may also generate some anxiety as you embark on a new task or push yourself to meet a new group of people. The key, though, is practice, practice, practice. Your efforts will not be in vain, for you are rewiring your brain. Rename, reframe, and redirect. If you change your thinking about this anxiety or fear of failure into a challenge, you are already thinking more positively and handling fear and anxiety differently than in the past.

Many of us have had very sad, traumatic moments in our lives with painful memories. Perhaps you had an unhealthy childhood where you desperately wanted a hero to come save you from your pain. *You can be your own hero.* You can heal your brain, and you can be a hero in your relationships. Taking the high ground is not easy, but it's worth it.

20.
The Brains Worst Enemy

Please keep in mind that stress is one of the greatest enemies of the brain. Periods of prolonged stress increase your levels of cortisol and adrenaline, causing malfunctions across the human system. Cortisol alone encourages weight gain which is the least of your worries. It impedes neuron development and *increases synaptic pruning across ALL neural pathways.*

Stress can cause brain damage.

In a constant state of stress, your poor brain cannot build neurons or replace them. And when we say prolonged periods, we don't mean years of excessive stress. Studies have shown that feeling stressed for even more than an hour will cause the brain to begin to prune back the number of its branches, and therefore synaptic connections of hippocampal neurons.

As stress continues, the unhealthy conditions will also increase the rate of cell death in regions of the brain, reducing the capacity for contextual memory. After a long day of stressful work, you may find yourself making silly mistakes or forgetting basic things. Or if you have been working on a difficult problem for a long time, you may find an obvious answer to the problem after walking away from the stress and returning to it in a few hours. This is no coincidence.

This is why stress reduction techniques are so important – such as a hot bath with lavender Epsom salt, progressive muscle relaxation, exercise, deep breathing, or meditation. Often times just taking a break can relieve an enormous amount of stress. There are a variety of stress reduction techniques – do some research and find out which ones' work best for you.

21.
Steps to a New Life

As with anything, the first step is to become aware of the awesome power that you have available to you. The second step is to create habits that will help you get to where you want to go and be who you want to be. The third step is to believe that what you are about to embark upon does have significant benefit for you, and that you will reap those benefits once you start to take action. The one thing that your subconscious is good at is calculating cost to benefit ratios. Your brain wants to give you what it thinks you want. The familiar. If you are about to embark on something extremely difficult, or challenging, you may find your subconscious trying to sabotage you internally, which excuses, justifications, and such. This is one of the reasons many people fail at trying to elevate themselves - because they do not believe in what they are doing, and they do not have the facts to prove it to themselves. The currency between your conscious and your subconscious is desire and belief. If you have sufficient amounts of those, your subconscious will be on board. The key is to become aware of this internal programming. Once you are aware of it, you can start redirecting your brain to go where you what it to go. You can be the Captain of your ship. You can easily influence your brain by telling it why you want to steer it a certain way.

For example, let's say you go out to eat with a friend, to celebrate a huge accomplishment. Your brain wants to order a frozen mudslide and French fries. It doesn't care that those two things combined will be 1600 calories. It wants you to celebrate! And it knows mudslides are your favorite drink. It wants you to have what you want. So, you go back and forth internally. You know that you are only 5 pounds away from your goal weight, but this is a huge, once in a lifetime accomplishment. You deserve it, but you know you should have water. Whenever you find yourself struggling internally, become aware, pause, take a deep breath, and remind yourself that you are the Captain of your ship. All you have to do is tell your brain why you think water will be best. Seriously, it's like talking to a child. And, of course, you can do this silently, inside your head. Just explain that you appreciate it wanting to give you what it thinks you want, but it's coming from default mode and that you no longer want to be coming from that place. Water has zero calories, and you are not going to sabotage yourself when you are this close to your goal. Your brain will be like oh, okay, I get it. I'm starting to understand. Yes, that makes sense. And the more you do this, the more this will become familiar to the brain. Each time you create new and stronger neurons which will make this the norm for you. You can do this with any goal that you have, big or small. The brain doesn't care. It's amazing! So, with these three elements of understanding - becoming aware, creating new habits and neuron connections, and believing it will benefit you - it is now time to layout some simple steps you can take to reach your goals.

Reflection

Your first step is sincere and deep reflection. When you do deep reflection, you are actually identifying the neurons, the pathways that the neurons form, and the bunch or networks that all point to the area that you want to change or redirect. Of course, you will not be cognizant of where these neurons are and what they look like. Your brain automatically takes care of that for you. All you have to do is think about the areas in your life that you want to change or improve.

Reflection doesn't require any special skill except honesty and the ability to trace your steps from the things that you have been responsible for, to the lot in life you currently experience. Taking full responsibility for your life is huge. It can be so easy to blame others, but that will get us nowhere fast.

"It's not your fault if you were born poor. But if you die poor, it is your fault." Bill Gates

Of course, Bill Gates is rich, but I don't think this quote necessarily has to focus on money. We can be poor in spirit, health, wealth, friendships, relationships, etc. Once we realize what we don't want, we are responsible for changing it.

"Don't complain about things you're not willing to change." ~ Unknown

The person who will be successful in reflection is the person who will be brutally honest with himself and who will take full responsibility for all of the things that happen and have happened to him. You see, without taking responsibility you will not be able to control it in the future and if you do not control that element in the future you will not be able to change your destiny.

The moment you start with reflection and you start telling yourself that you are going to, from this day forth, take responsibility for your actions, you will have already started to change the neural pathways that govern your outlook on life.

After repeatedly telling yourself this, you will find that it will start to become your reality and it will become easier and easier. You will be able to reach deeper to find the areas that you need to identify, reshape, and redirect to move you towards the life that you are in search of.

In the process of reflection, the first step is to decide what you want. The second step is to find out what is blocking you from getting there. You are essentially trying to plot a map that shows where you are and where you want to go. This, and the desire to take responsibility for your life, will get the process of neuroplasticity working in your favor. Desire and belief, as we said, are two things that you truly need, to get yourself in the game.

Asking

Your second step is the process of asking. When you ask, and you ask repeatedly, your subconscious starts to automatically take all the things you know, whether you are aware of it or not, and it starts to plot a path to where you need to be. Asking is a powerful tool and you should never discount the power of questions. Questions make you think of things you haven't thought of before. Questions open doors that would stay shut otherwise. Questions allow you to figure out what you really want and help you move toward your goals. Questions help you learn from others.

Meditation

Meditation has been proven to place the brain in such perfect states that neuroplasticity is promoted aggressively. In the same way that meditation can be of aid, focused sleep can do the same thing. Focused sleep works best when you tire yourself out with a high-level workout. This means that you workout to get the necessary neurotransmitters pumping. With vigorous workout, you will get your body to release hormones that promote deep sleep.

Before you sleep, conduct your reflection, ask your questions, and begin your short meditation. Make sure you keep your meditation focused and not blank. There are two kinds of meditation. One is to keep your mind absolutely blank and let your subconscious take over. The other kind of meditation is to increase your brain's conscious capacity by concentrating intently on just one thing, in this case concentrate on the thing that you are asking for.

When you desire, believe, ask, and meditate you set up the necessary elements for your brain to deliberately form strong neurons which will steer you in the right direction. No other method can produce faster and longer lasting results.

There is one impediment to this, however, that most people are not aware of. If in the process of reflecting and asking, you are confused and unsure about what you want, your brain will not be able to create the changes needed to the existing pathways. It is the way nature protects us from flighty and transient fancies. You must, first, decide and be extremely clear about what it is that you want. For short-term changes, you can change habits, but for long-term changes, you have to deliberately reprogram your default mind, and you do this by utilizing your plastic brain.

It is important that you understand the way your mind works, and the way neuroplasticity works within the different parts of your mental processes. You will see discernable changes after you consistently practice all that you've learned here.

Your brain is adaptable and changeable. This is a proven fact. What you choose to take in will form neuro pathways and the more you focus on something, good or bad, the stronger that pathway becomes. Who you surround yourself with, what you watch and listen to, what you think, and the words you speak out of your own mouth creates your destiny. But you have a choice! If you become deliberate with what you allow in, and what you focus on and think about, then positive and beneficial neuro pathways will be formed and strengthened, which will automatically produce desired results. It's so exciting! You just have to take action and follow through.

22.
Simple Practices You Can Do Right Now

Your brain is adaptable, and you can change it yourself! You are literally capable of rewiring your brain and anyone can do it! You can reprogram your brain. Choose what you want and who you want to be and then start rewiring your brain to get the results that you want. Here are some simple practices that you can do right now to start rewiring your brain in a positive way. Life is supposed to be enjoyable and amazing, and it can be! The key is to keep at it. Do not allow outside forces to shape your brain in negative ways. Don't' fall back into your comfort zone. Do not fall back into your old ways and habits. You've got this! Decide, discover, and learn what it is that you want to wire. The next step is to take action. What you have learned now needs to be applied.

Simple practices:

- Start your day right. Positive morning rituals. Gratitude.
- Imagine what you want in detail. Utilize your imagination. Especially before bed.

- Be present, focus, observe.
- Generate the feeling you want more of.
- Make lists and take action.
- Gratitude journal.
- Only speak about what you want. Only let positive words come out of your mouth.
- Meditate and breathe (doesn't have to be for long)
- Affirmations that feel good.
- Always find the good in every situation. Flat tire? Maybe the delay saved you from getting in an accident. We can't see the big picture. Find the good and trust.
- Always find the good in everyone. Do not think or speak negatively about anyone. These thoughts and feelings will hinder and negatively affect you, instead.
- Mirror work (Say "I am" affirmations while looking in the mirror. I am successful. I am prosperous. I am healthy. I am loving. I am perfect just the way I am, etc.)
- Exercise: bike, skip, jump-rope, swim, do jumping jacks, dance. Have fun with it.
- Be happy. Don't worry about what anyone thinks. Some people are uptight and clearly haven't learned how to let loose and have fun. Don't worry about people who can't truly enjoy life. Laugh, be silly, and be happy.

Repetition, repetition, repetition.

Repetition is the key. And we know that everything starts with a thought. Thoughts are powerful. Thoughts become things. Thoughts inspire action. Thoughts generate different emotions. The more you are deliberate with what you are thinking, the more your life will change in the direction that you want it to. You get to choose. Once you learn this, you will no longer have to linger in a negative default mode. Do not waste a thought. Your thoughts and what you think determine everything in your life. Do not waste a single thought. As with everything, it takes practice, but it will be so worth it in the end. Believe it or not, you are in control of what you think about. It may not feel that way if you've been in a negative default mode for a long time, but it is completely true. You get to choose what you think about. And all you have to do is practice replacing random, default mode thoughts with intentional, purposeful, and beneficial thoughts. Do this for at least 30 days, straight. You cannot skip a day. If you accidently forget to be deliberate one day, you will need to start your 30 days over. I know this may sound a bit over the top, but again, it's worth it. You have nothing to lose and everything to gain.

Everything you deliberately, and everything you do not deliberately, put into your brain effects the outcome of your life, therefore, you are going to have to be careful what you allow in. What goes on around you is creating and forming neural pathways in your brain whether you know it or not. For example, the majority of the news is negative; therefore, it shouldn't be allowed to enter in. Yes, you may have formed a habit of watching the nightly news before bed, but if it will not benefit you in a positive, uplifting way, then it needs to go. Studies have shown that people who stop watching the news tend to be happier and healthier. If you have a friend who is always negative, then you may need to distance yourself from them. They have simply formed strong connections in the brain around negativity and now it is habitual for them. Until they are ready to make new connections, you can't subject yourself to it. If you do, you too, will be creating new and strong connections around being negative. Negativity will become a learned trait, even if you don't like it or agree with it, your subconscious mind records and stores everything it experiences. Period.

Conclusion

Your brain is adaptable. You can rewire your brain to think and do things that will benefit you in all areas of your life, especially your future. This concept actually has double the benefits because the Law of Attraction states that you get what you think about. So, not only can you rewire your brain so that your default mode is positive, but in doing so you will also be utilizing the Law of Attraction. No longer will your feelings tell you how to feel, but you will learn how to master your feelings. You will tell your feelings how to feel, and with practice, it will become a positive habit.

The main reason people fail to make this proven science work for them is because they don't make it a long-term habit. It's easier to be in a default mode that has been formed unconsciously, but it is definitely not better.

So be deliberate and keep at it. You can change your beliefs with awareness and repetition.

The ramifications of neuroplasticity are far reaching and still being studied. But the simple fact that our brains are in a constant state of flux, changing with every thought, and adapting to maximize what it believes its best function is, is truly humbling. Even if you don't decide to try any of the tips we have provided to enhance your positive neuroplasticity, it is our sincere hope that we have delivered a positive message to you with our exploration of the concept. Life is yours for the taking. Very little can hold you back, once you learn how your brain really works.

It has been my goal to show you the rationalization of a simple process that can help you determine the course of the rest of your life.

You need to understand the basics of the brain's workings so that you can absorb the sea of data and columns of commentary out there explaining everything from the basics of neurogenesis, to neuroplasticity and to be able to sift through what is plausible from what is unreliable.

But if you want to put aside all the scientific jargon and just drill down to the actionable intelligence that is contained amidst the lines of this book then you need focus on just three things.

First, you need to be able to reflect honestly and without interruption. Reflection, even though it seems to be thrown about aimlessly in today's metaphysical industry, holds a very powerful part of the human evolution and the story of our development. There is no doubt that each of us is trying to be better at one thing or another.

If you can't see why reflection is important to the growth of your psychological self and your material gain in this world, think about the analogy of the map. If you had no idea where you are, I could give you the most detailed 3-D map and the location of the world's largest trove of precious treasure, and you would have no way of getting to it, if you did not know where you were. That is exactly what reflection does.

It seeks to alert your consciousness to things your

subconscious already knows. But you need to alert your conscious mind, because it is your conscious mind that is making the decision to go on the quest for that treasure. In your case, the treasure happens to be the most powerful thing known to man, and that is the ability to get whatever he truly desires.

To be successful and to attain what your heart desires you must have a certain mindset that will allow you to make all the right moves in response to each situation and stimuli. How you react to something is just as important as how you act in the absence of an external stimuli. This pattern of reaction and this mindset of responses is all neatly mapped out in your neural pathways.

But not everything that is mapped out is something that you did or what you wanted. Sometimes it was just environmental forces that forced you to react in a certain way and that reaction took hold of how you do things, today. But, upon reflection, you realize that needs to be changed. Or, in another way, you could have been involved in a horrific experience that changed the way you see things or the way you respond to things, and that too, is a function of the neurological pathways that developed without your permission. To shake off those chains, you need to know that those pathways can be altered, even erased, given sufficient time and effort; because the brain is designed to evolve and cope. It has a process of neuroplasticity and it allows you to alter the echoes of the past so that you can determine the beat of your future.

To change your life, you have to want it. The brain responds to desire and belief. If you desire something, it means that which you desire is already yours, you just have to work at getting it. And one of the first things you need to do is have the mindset that you can absolutely, without question, do what is needed to get it done.

When you want it bad enough, the pathways of your brain begin to alter, to the point that it needs to be able to put you within striking distance of what you need. Once you reflect and you begin to understand your strengths and weaknesses you will be able to curb your weaknesses and fortify your strengths from a neurological perspective.

Once you have reflected, then the process of asking, repeatedly, that which you want and desire, goes on to fortify those neurons and the connections that it needs to make. Each path is strengthened, and each path is bolstered with redundant neurons to make sure that, in case of injury, you are left with an alternate neurological path to your objective. You will find that the things most important to you are not easy to forget. But the things that are not, can be easily forgotten.

If you were to draw an analogy of creating your dreams and forging a sword, the first two steps of reflecting and asking would be like the steps of shaping the steel and hammering it. If you want to really make that sword strong, you still have one more step to do, you have to fire it in the furnace. You need to subject it to a force that brings it together and casts it in a way that it is unshakable and unbreakable.

This is what meditation does. Meditation has been repeatedly proven to alter and redraw the lines of the pathways and get you to the point of renewing yourself from who you were to who you want to be. Being in a constant state of meditation is a great way to super sharpen your focus and operate at a highly effective and efficient level.

Reflect. Ask. Meditate. These are all you need to form a

functional perspective to alter the neurological pathways of your brain to not only become successful, but also to become the definition of success.

And, once again, here are a few simple practices you can do to get started right now. Have fun and enjoy a more enjoyable life! You deserve it!

Simple practices:

- Start your day right. Positive morning rituals. Gratitude.
- Imagine what you want in detail. Utilize your imagination. Especially before bed.
- Be present, focus, observe.
- Generate the feeling you want more of.
- Make lists and take action.
- Gratitude journal.
- Only speak about what you want. Only let positive words come out of your mouth.
- Meditate and breathe (doesn't have to be for long)
- Affirmations that feel good.
- Always find the good in every situation. Flat tire? Maybe the delay saved you from getting in an accident. We can't see the big picture. Find the good and trust.
- Always find the good in everyone. Do not think or speak negatively about anyone. These thoughts and feelings will hinder and negatively affect you, instead.
- Mirror work (Say "I am" affirmations while looking in the mirror. I am successful. I am prosperous. I am healthy. I am loving. I am perfect just the way I am, etc.)
- Exercise: bike, skip, jump-rope, swim, do jumping jacks, dance. Have fun with it.
- Be happy. Don't worry about what anyone thinks. Some people are uptight and clearly haven't learned

how to let loose and have fun. Don't worry about people who can't truly enjoy life. Laugh, be silly, and be happy.

Repetition, repetition, repetition.

About Sage Wilcox

Sage lives in the United States and is a certified energy healer. Sage enjoys giving advice to clients, friends, and family on healing, love, and relationships. Sage also enjoys studying human behavior, reading, writing, being outdoors, and enhancing her relationships with others.

Other books by Sage Wilcox:

- *Love Letters from Exes: Proof That Life Goes On After a Break Up and Love Is What You Make It*

- *Get It Up: 101 Ways to Raise Your Vibration, Reduce Stress, Depression, & Anxiety, Increase Joy, Peace, & Happiness and Attract Abundance Automatically!*

- *The 2-Hour Vacation: Let Go and Relax, Reduce Stress & Anxiety, Gain Inner Peace, and Happiness*

- *Until We Fall (A Romance Novel)*

- *The Importance of Doing It: How to Utilize Discipline to Get Out of Bed, and Make Your Dreams Come True! A Guide to Taking Action to Create Successful Habits, Reduce Stress, Anxiety, & Depression & Gain Self-Discipline, Motivation, & Success!*

- *Less Is Best: Declutter, Organize, & Simplify to Reach Minimalism; Get More Time, Money, & Energy*

- *You Had Me at Re: Hello: The Ultimate Guide to Online Dating, Including Tips and Testimonies*

Please consider leaving a review and visit her at:
http://sagewilcox.wix.com/books
www.facebook.com/sagewilcoxbooks
Thank you!

Disclaimer

The purpose of this book is for entertainment purposes only. This book is designed to provide information and motivation to our readers. The content of each article, letter, or insight is the sole expression and opinion of its author, and not necessarily that of the publisher. The letters contained in this book are from contributors and are the contributor's recollections of their experiences. This is a work based on opinions, recollections, and true events, however, names, characters, businesses, places, and incidents are either the products of the authors' imaginations or used in a fictitious manner. Any resemblance to actual persons, living or dead, businesses, companies, events, locales, or actual events is entirely coincidental. This book is not intended nor is it implied to be a substitute for professional medical advice, and any medical advice and any medical information contained in this book is not intended to be diagnostic or treatment in any way. The author and publisher are not engaged in rendering medical, psychological, legal, or any other professional services. If medical, psychological or other expert assistance is required, please talk to your physician and locate the services of a competent professional. The author and publisher shall have neither liability nor responsibility to any person or entity with respect to any loss or damage caused, or alleged to have been caused, directly or indirectly, by the information contained in this book. Neither the publisher nor the individual author(s) shall be liable for any physical, psychological, emotional, financial, or commercial damages, including, but not limited to, special, incidental, consequential or other damages. Our views and rights are the same: You are responsible for your own choices, actions, and results. If you do not wish to be bound by the above, you may return this book along with a copy of the receipt to the publisher for a full refund.

www.ingramcontent.com/pod-product-compliance
Lightning Source LLC
Chambersburg PA
CBHW061446040426
42450CB00007B/1238